Electric Guitars & Basses 2002-2006

By Michael Tonn

ISBN: 978-1-157424-4205
SAN 683-8022

Copyright © 2024 CENTERSTREAM Publishing
P.O. Box 17878 - Anaheim Hills, CA 92817

www.centerstream-usa.com | centerstrm@aol.com | 714-779-9390

All rights for publication and distribution are reserved. No part of this book may be reproduced in any form or by any Electronic or mechanical means including information storage and retrieval systems without permission in writing from the publisher, except by reviewers who may quote brief passages in review.

This book is in no way intended to infringe on the intellectual property rights of any party. All products, brands, and names represented are trademarks or registered trademarks of their perspective companies; information in this book was derived from the author's independent research and was not authorized, furnished or approved by other parties.

Fingerprints

Fender is unique, even among its class of great American brands. Its influence on the sound, fashion and symbolism of contemporary music is undeniable. The passion for this iconic American brand among its devoted followers is unparalleled. Yes, people love Apple, Amazon and Tesla, but they don't tattoo the brand logos on their bodies, pose with their laptop in wedding photos or ask to be buried with their car. This is hallowed ground reserved for brands that have defined our lives. Brands like Fender. No pressure here for those who choose to carry the flag!

I suspect it may be difficult for many people to imagine what it's like to land a dream gig working for a really cool storied American brand that happens to make the very guitars and amps one already uses and loves. I'm not talking about a great position in a fast-moving growth industry. I'm talking bona fide, mic-drop, how did I get here, Dream Gig. That position you never would have imagined you would have, in a million years. A role that chooses *you*, and completely upends the traditional hunt for career fulfillment. Mike Tonn is one of the few that knows this journey firsthand.

Being the "guitar guy" at Fender isn't always a walk in the park. If it was an easy job, it wouldn't have been so cool. The passion for the brand creates an extraordinarily high level of expectation and concern from its loyal fans. I've joked before that when I brought a new color to market my mother would call and ask "if I was sure it was the right move?" Whimsical, but not that far from the truth.

Mike navigated these waters on a global level to define the products that would elevate the brand, inspire individuality, and sustain Fender's recaptured relevance. Conversations with customers, influential artists, dealers, foreign distributors, sales and marketing teams, factories—a seemingly endless stream of input, needs and preferences to evaluate and resolve. It all had to be considered in the product line definition.

As I reviewed the body of work Mike has meticulously reconstructed here, I was blown away not only by the shear number of products introduced, but also by the depth of creativity and innovation that emerged during this period. I recall feeling new pressure to respond to a rapidly fragmenting market. It was a new season of specialization that would rapidly evolve to become an era of personalization. The teams had their noses to the grindstone, busily, ideating, developing, and launching instruments to inspire a new field of creative musicians. So many captivating and innovative guitars defining a new generation of relevance. I've truthfully never had the opportunity to review this rich season in its entirety, until now.

Mike has assembled here the most comprehensive record of new Fender guitar releases during this rich four-year period of development. I can imagine collectors and serious enthusiasts will sing its praises. Honestly, Mike is likely the only individual that could accurately pull this information together and share the backstories as well. This collection of guitars and basses is Mike's body of work within this legendary brand.

As you read this, I would ask you to take a step back, from the in-depth, model by model details Mike has compiled here for just a moment. I believe it's important to see this work in its true creative spirit. This is not just an assortment of products, features and specifications. It's more akin to the metaphoric cave paintings Maslow describes in his hierarchy of needs. These products are the expression of a purposeful, creative journey. The fingerprints and images of an artistic servant, the actualization of a man's creative vision, journey and focus. From all of us that call Fender ours: thank you Mike!

Richard McDonald retired **FMIC Chief Product Strategist**

INTRODUCTION

The reason I decided to write this book was truthfully a selfish one. I wanted to document a portion of my life that truly meant the most to me in terms of a musical career. Sure, I've played professionally for years, written and recorded albums, was a hired gun as a session player and in my earlier years pursued the dream of becoming a recording artist, but as tends to be the case with so many musicians, it never really managed to the pay bills, so I had to find a way to make a living within the industry that I grew up in. After I left Fender®, I thought back on my experiences there and felt that perhaps it might be fun to write about just what Fender was thinking at the time they released the instruments that they did. And who better to document those events than the person responsible for overseeing the ideas behind them? My business card had my name and the title was Marketing Manager Electric Guitar & Basses so that was precisely my job. Although this book only covers a short period of Fender's history, it does cover the who, what and why of the release of Fender guitars and basses from 2002-2006. This book provides insight (from the inside) into what was happening at that time with the largest guitar company in the world.

The purpose of this book is to give you, the consumer or Fender fan some insight into the models and thinking behind the models that were introduced during the years 2002-2006. Why Fender did what they did and what was conceived for the global marketplace to fulfill the desires of the consumer? Writing this book was a labor of love for me. I hope you like reading it as much as I enjoyed writing it.

The global marketing manager for Fender electric guitars & basses. It certainly sounds impressive, but one might naturally ask, "what does that mean and what does the person do who has that job?" Ultimately the role determines the assortment of Fender electric guitars and basses carried worldwide, and strategically manages the introduction of new products into the market. Sounds exciting? Clearly for a guitar enthusiast such as myself, it was an opportunity of a lifetime! It allowed me to be *creative* with Fender guitars and basses and carry on the Fender legacy of Leo Fender. That's what I did and that was the gig. Getting to be the Fender Electric Guitar "guy" was nothing short of an honor. That was my job. I started in 2001 as the Squier® and strategic brand marketing manager and in 2003 I was asked to take over Fender. At Fender, we all worked together as a team bouncing ideas and concepts off one another to come up with the best possible solution to satisfy the needs of the consumer and (ultimately the company). The vast amount of knowledge among the people at Fender still amazes me and what I learned during the time I worked there is etched in my mind forever. It was truly a life changing experience. I still think about and communicate with my family of friends at Fender. The people at Fender truly are a family. I'll never forget the day that I was in my office just a few days after I had started work there. I had just driven a thousand miles, left my family behind and felt alone at my new job in Scottsdale Arizona. Bill Schultz, owner and CEO of the company came into my office and "suggested" that he and his wife Mary Jane come by my apartment after work, pick me up, take me to dinner and then to a Diamondback baseball game. Brilliant, driven and compassionate. That's the man I remember in Bill Schultz.

That's what he expected out of the people that worked for him. That's the kind of family that Fender was. By the way, the Diamondbacks won the World Series that year.

FENDER® The Company

The Fender corporate offices are located in Scottsdale Arizona. The USA manufacturing facility is in Corona California while the Mexico manufacturing facility is located in Ensenada, Mexico. These operations are state of the art North America manufacturing plants with the best people in the world building guitars. Although the majority of Fender guitars come from these facilities, guitars were also sourced from Fender Japan and Korea during this time. All Fender guitars are overseen during manufacture by Fender plant specialists who know and understand how to build Fender guitars. These individuals are instrumental in making sure that the highest standards are met. Any Fender product manufactured has to be approved by the Fender marketing manager, regardless of where it is made or where in the world it is distributed.

The Process

Developing new instruments for Fender starts out like anything else. With an idea. The ideas are frequently spawned by market research. It only makes sense, right? Look at what people are into, what people are asking for, what new technology can be used in the production process and what is needed to round out the product assortment. "Is there a customer that would get excited about this product"? Again, it all starts with the idea. In addition, product development inspiration at a company with a history and heritage such as Fender's can frequently be more an exercise of exploring accurate reissues of iconic models. There's an ever-present demand for old guitars not only as collectible pieces, but also because of the unique designs and features of the instruments themselves. Back when I was a kid, I remember wanting that '72 Strat® in the music store window ... but could only dream of buying a $350 guitar like that. Now, of course, buying a reissue of that very guitar I wanted as a kid is an attainable goal. When considering the reissue of an instrument I always started with eBay, to see what the original models were selling for and if it looked like there was obvious demand for these obsolete instruments. With Fender factories in California, Mexico and Japan, there are numerous opportunities to make new products and or reproduce old ones. The Japanese in particular are every bit as astute when it comes to Fender heritage and Fender models as Americans are. Once the idea was born, the next step was to fly to the factory in Corona and sit down with the head of R & D (research and development), who for many years was Dan Smith. Dan had been with Fender since 1981 and gave new meaning to the phrase "seasoned veteran"; his wealth of knowledge and Fender history was second to none. I learned much about Fender from Dan and enjoyed working closely with him. Working with Dan taught me what could or could not be achieved in manufacturing and the reasoning why.

As time went on, I honed my skills when it came to requesting products that could actually be realistically produced. If it *couldn't* be produced, it was usually because we didn't have the proper tooling to make it. In the case of Eric Johnson's Strat, for example, we had to secure approval directly from Bill Schultz to buy the tooling needed to build Eric's guitar. That in turn meant that because of this significant upfront investment, we would have to sell a large number of these models and plan to amortize these costs over the coming years.

In any case, once a product's manufacturing feasibility has been established — and it's been confirmed that demand does (or likely will) exist for the product in question, the next step in the process is to create a sample. This "sample" was then typically built in the model shop in Corona based off of the specifications compiled by myself or Dan Smith. In some cases, if it was a re-creation of an older model, I would locate an actual example of the instrument in question and purchase it. In other cases, purchasing a physical example was unnecessary as we were able to locate the original drawings and reference files dating from when it was first produced. And in other instances, it was simply more of a "brainstorming" approach, sitting down with Dan and a group of Fender veterans and just seeing what we could come up with real-time. This book covers each model in the order they were introduced. Typically, new models were introduced twice a year: either in January at the Winter NAMM show in Anaheim, or in July at the Summer NAMM show in Nashville. At each of these shows, a new pricelist was made available which included all of the new models. While not *every* new model was introduced at these trade shows, the vast majority were. Other instruments such as factory special run models ("FSR's") were introduced throughout the year, but these were only available through specific channels and in limited quantities. This book covers the models that I contributed to, oversaw, and/or was responsible for, with the obvious "credit where due" to the many, many talented individuals on the Fender team who similarly helped support their successful introduction. When I first became responsible for Fender electric guitars and basses, I picked up where my predecessor (Richard McDonald) had left off — and when I left the company, I similarly handed the reins over to Justin Norvell. meaning "job one" was essentially to take on our predecessors' creations and see them through to production.

And so my stories begins.

Nashville: July 2002

Nashville: July 2004

Anaheim: January 2005

Nashville: July 2005

Anaheim: January 2006

Finishes-What Was Used and Why?

I won't get into *tremendous* detail here about the types of finishes that were used, as that information is easily attainable. That said, I'll cover here the basics of the Fender finishes that were available for us to use at the time — as well as some of the pros and cons of each selection.

Polyester

This finish was used primarily in our Mexico factory because it was easy to spray and once cured, could be polished to a very durable, high-gloss finish. These qualities made polyester finishes a natural choice for mass-produced, lower cost instruments. Polyester finishes are very durable, tough and hard to scratch, dent and or damage.

Poly Urethane

Polyurethane was and still is a tougher, more weather-and chemical-resistant process when compared to acrylic lacquer. "Poly," as it's called, is still one of the most commonly used finishes on electric instruments. It allows for more resonant frequencies from the instrument when compared to polyester, and as a result this finish was used in most of the US factory production line instruments.

Acrylic lacquer

This finish helped cut down on process time, requiring less buffing to obtain a shine. It was very quick-drying and helped keep costs down relative to other finishes applied in the US factory. It was used primarily on the Highway One series of instruments at the time.

Nitrocellulose lacquer

Many players with great "ears" can listen closely to the resonant frequencies of the instrument — "acoustically" without the instrument plugged in — and hear the distinctive "ringing" of the wood in an instrument finished with nitrocellulose lacquer. The only downside to "nitro," as it's called, is that it is a rather delicate finish. But it tends to age like a fine wine, meaning in musical sense, it only sounds better and better with age.

Thin Skin Lacquer

The only difference between "Thin Skin" lacquer and Nitrocellulose lacquer was in the name. When we made instruments for Japan, more times than not, their request was

"Thin Skin Lacquer". This meant a thinner layer of color and a thinner layer of the clear top-coat that was applied. It took a true skilled painter to do this. After the finished cured, it also required much care and detail in the buffing and polishing process.

Color Selection

How the finish was applied was one thing, but how colors were decided upon and formulated was quite another. We all know that the color palette for electric instruments has continued to widen and evolve through the years. Consider that there were only a few colors used back in the '50s on Fender® instruments. We saw those change and expand in the early '60s as muscle cars began to enter the market.

When I initially came on board at Fender, I realized there was a need to outright educate myself on historic and current practices in order to help continue shaping what was to come. Thankfully, I had access to many of the best in the business to teach me.

When it came to colors, I went back to the roots: car companies. Typically, car companies have complex business plans in the development of new models, 5-7 years in advance of the model before it is released. That means they are looking at potential colors at that time as well. I ended up making a contact with a person at Lexus (Toyota) who shall remain nameless, after many phone calls. He was a guitar player, owned a Fender and knew what was planned in the way of models for his car company. Though he could not disclose any specific information, he was able to "name drop" a few colors. I kept a close eye on what new car colors were coming out when announcements were made prior to when models were introduced (usually the prior fall of the upcoming year) and since we could react fairly quickly, I ran with new colors in this way. Blizzard Pearl would be an example of a color we introduced in August of 2004 with the Cyclone® HH guitar. The history of Fender's manufacturing is well documented and available so I will not go into any of that. My stories are the focus of the models in my career at Fender.

Nashville: July 2002

Artist Series Buddy Guy Polka Dot Stratocaster® - It goes without saying that Buddy Guy is an electric guitar legend. Upon his arrival in Chicago in1957 Buddy quickly made his mark and became a session player at the legendary CHESS recording studios. Stage shows were jaw dropping. Buddy used every trick in the book and invented just as many himself. His talent didn't stop there either, as he was a brilliant showman and a gifted singer as well. Buddy's guitar of choice back then? His '50s Fender Stratocaster.

We at Fender could not have been more proud to work with the man who has been cited as the guitar hero of Jimi Hendrix, Eric Clapton, Stevie Ray Vaughan and Gary Clark Jr, just to name a few. Buddy's signature model became his Polka Dot Strat® made in our Mexico factory. Buddy was thrilled to have his own model and is seen playing it in nearly every performance photo. This Stratocaster was similar to a standard Strat with a few "Buddy tweaks". It featured an alder body, soft V-shaped one-piece maple neck, 21 medium jumbo frets, three standard ceramic single-coil Strat pickups and vintage-style tremolo and tuning machines.

It's not every guitar player that wants his Fender signature guitar covered in polka dots. I had to ask about his motivation for the desired design. Buddy sat in my office and told me the reason he wanted a Polka Dot Stratocaster was to honor his mother and, in a roundabout way, fulfill a promise he had made her. Buddy had promised his mother that he was going to buy her a polka dot Cadillac when he hit it big with his musical career. The Cadillac purchase never happened, but in tribute to his mom, the guitar did. Later we made additional versions of this guitar. Red, with White polka dots and White with Black polka dots.

American Special Series Toronado® - The Toronado was an original patented body design by Fender®. It was first produced in our Mexico factory in 1998 and its popularity inspired the USA version which was released in July of 2002. It has a totally different look from other Fender models, its eye catching and yet still unmistakably "Fender".

The "Toronado Special" as it was called came in two different pickup configurations. The Crimson Transparent example (shown left) is equipped with two Atomic II humbuckers that delivered a warm full-throated tone. The Butterscotch Blonde model (shown right) is fitted with twin P-90 style single-coil pickups that were still able to deliver fat solo tones but with more "edge" for articulate rhythm playing. These guitars featured mahogany bodies for a rich full sound and were fitted with 24 ¾" scale necks. The bridge designs were very unique, featuring Fender's Adjust-o-matic™ bridges and stop tail pieces.

These two guitars were both available in Butterscotch Blonde & Crimson Transparent. Although its production was short lived it was quite effective. We were able to demonstrate that Fender could produce a different-sounding and playing instrument while still preserving the Fender look and tradition. These guitars were unique in tone and feel with their mahogany bodies and shorter scale lengths. All versions of the Toronado were discontinued in 2007. One has to assume, not unlike other Fender models that have come and gone, that this model is bound to be another sought-after Fender collectible.

Deluxe Series Cyclone® II - The original Fender® Cyclone was introduced in July of 1998 and was a new model for Fender at the time. It was a bit of a mash-up of a Jaguar and a Mustang. The body was more 'Mustang-y' but with a Strat® style tremolo, and the neck was 24 ¾" scale length with the "big headstock" common to both models at various times in their production. The original Cyclone also held some similarities to the Jag-Stang® introduced in 1996. Fender had such great ideas that it was frequently tempting to borrow some of the features of one guitar and combine them with another.

The Deluxe Series Cyclone II was introduced in 2002 to the existing Cyclone family of guitars. What really set the Cyclone II apart from its predecessors was its three vintage style Jaguar® single-coil chrome steel sided pickups. Another eye-catching feature was the Jaguar style chrome plate that had individual on-off switches for each pickup.

Of course, it *had* to have a racing stripe, since Fender® had always been a Southern California-based company, Hot Rods and surfing were always considered part of the foundational culture of Fender. The traditional racing stripe we used was also a nod to the Fender "Competition Mustang" guitars of the late '60s and '70s. We retained the 24 ¾" scale length neck, resulting in a uniquely different playing feel and sound when compared to a traditional 3 pickup Stratocaster® or two pickup Jaguar.

The Cyclone Series endured for almost 10 years but was discontinued in 2007. More recently, a new variant of the Cyclone II (featuring Stratocaster pickups) did re-enter the scene in 2020 as part of Squier's Paranormal Series.

Deluxe Series Competition Mustang® - The Mustang made its debut in 1964. Not unlike the single pickup Musicmaster® (1955) and the double pickup Duo-Sonic® (1956), the Mustang was basically designed to capture the eye of the "student" market. This is why these models were a little smaller and featured a 24-inch scale length neck, shorter than traditional Fender® models. (The original Music Master and Duo-Sonic models were even shorter, with 22 ½" scale length necks.) The model featured two purpose-built Mustang single-coil pickups and a floating bridge with "Dynamic" vibrato tail-piece; maple neck with rosewood fingerboard; vintage style tuning machines; an on/off slider, in/out of phase switch for each pickup; with a master volume and tone control.

The first Competition Mustang was released by Fender back in 1969 when muscle cars were at the peak of their popularity. We reissued this Deluxe Series Competition Mustang guitar only for a few months in 2002. At that time our Fender Mustang guitars were being manufactured in the Japanese factory and many of Japan's production models came with matching headstocks — the ask here was outside the norm. My reissue of the Competition Mustang, complete with racing stripe, was designed to replicate the original spec as closely as possible. Although initially viewed as a student model by many, the Mustang has proven to be a professional performance grade instrument for its entire history. The stock Mustang tremolo is wonderfully supple and effective, and the guitar's electronics have always sounded great.

Fender Mustangs are still being made in the Japanese factory at the time of this writing. Although the market for Mustangs in Japan is strong, the demand for these guitars is global and the Mustang remains yet another Fender iconic model.

The Deluxe Series Competition Mustang was available in Daphne Blue and Candy Apple Red and (of course) featured the competition racing stripe. These 2002 reissues are not easy to find because their life cycle was relatively short and not that many of them were built.

Artist Series Mark Hoppus Bass - Although Blink-182 began its rise to popularity in 1997, it wasn't until late 1999 that the world *really* began to take notice of what these guys from California were doing. The band has now sold more than 50 million records worldwide and is widely considered the vanguard of punk pop. The guys as individuals were super creative, brash, original — and they absolutely rocked.

Before starting at Fender®, I had been the electric guitar product manager and buyer for the largest online music retailer at the time: Musician's Friend. Fender was our largest guitar account and I handled the account personally; I was lucky enough to be able to quickly establish a great working relationship with everyone at Fender.

In 2001 I met Fender's Marketing Manager, Richard McDonald, at the Anaheim NAMM show — I was there to get a preview of Fender's new releases. I must confess at the time I had minimal familiarity with Blink-182, but Richard assured me that they were huge and convinced me to buy the brand-new Tom DeLonge Stratocaster for Musician's Friend. I did so and, long story short, Richard's advisement was spot-on: that guitar was incredibly successful for both Fender and Musician's Friend.

The next year, now as an employee for Fender, it made perfect sense to collaborate with Blink-182's talented bassist Mark Hoppus. Mark wanted a Jazz Bass® body but with a Precision Bass® neck. Simple but punchy: we loaded this bass with a single Seymour Duncan® Basslines Quarter Pound Precision Bass pickup, controlled by a single volume knob. Other features included a rosewood fingerboard, medium-jumbo frets with dot inlays and a uniquely shaped four-ply white pearloid pickguard.

Deluxe Series Mustang® Bass - In the summer of 2002, Fender brought the Mustang Bass back to the US market. The Mustang was originally made in the US from 1966 to 1982 and then had been discontinued. Interestingly enough, it was Leo Fender's final original bass design for Fender before he left the company in 1965.

Our factory in Japan has always produced guitars for a variety of markets worldwide, but not every model manufactured in Japan is imported into the United States. Fender Japan had started as a joint venture in 1982 between Kanda Shokai and Yamano Gakki, but with Fender's launch of Fender Music Corporation (Japan) in April of 2015 it has since assumed the Japanese business entirely.

We have frequently peppered a compelling variety of instruments made in Japan into the US market. Our Fender Japan factory has always manufactured first class instruments of superior quality. Further, Fender Japan has made a number of instruments that were truthfully not commonly seen in the US otherwise. The reason is that the Fender Japan factory had certain tooling and machinery that we did not have in our Corona, CA or Ensenada factories at the time. The original Mustang had been produced in Fullerton, CA and not Corona. Fact is, not all of Fullerton's machinery had been included in the in the CBS sale of Fender.

That said, as with other instruments you'll see in this book, we chose to bring models like this bass into the US market at different periods of time to satisfy consumer demand and bolster the diversity of our product offering.

The main feature of the Mustang Bass that makes it unique is the shorter scale length, not unlike that of the Mustang guitar. The Mustang bass has a 30" scale length — and when coupled with its smaller body, this truly is an ideal bass for students and players with smaller hands who tend to find the full-scale P and J Basses unwieldy. The instrument's bridge is unique to the model and allows intonation of each string, making it a fully professional instrument. The available colors were Fiesta Red with pearloid pickguard (shown here) and Vintage White with brown shell pickguard.

Anaheim: January 2003

Artist Series Robert Cray Stratocaster® - Robert Cray has long been known as a "Strat® guy" with his own signature Strat sound. A soulful performer and fantastic singer, Robert is the complete package. His signature Custom Shop Stratocaster (designed and built by the great Michael Stevens of Fender's Custom Shop) had been a special-order item since 1990. Robert's unmistakable clean, out-of-phase Stratocaster tone was achieved by lowering the guitar's pickups to the level of the pickguard.

In an effort to bring the Fender "magic" to the masses, we added Robert Cray's guitar, the Jimmy Vaughan Strat, and a few other signature series models to Fender's Mexico-manufactured Artist Series.

The Robert Cray Artist Series model featured three custom vintage Strat pickups and hardtail construction. We built very few Stratocaster guitars at that time with this hardtail bridge. The hardtail design dates back to the '50s when the Strat was offered "without Tremolo." It features a through-the-body stringing system much like a Telecaster; and there is no route in the body for a tremolo bridge.

In the last known photo taken of Stevie Ray Vaughan on August 26th, 1990, we see Eric Clapton, SRV, Jimmy Vaughan and Robert Cray backstage at the Alpine Valley Music Theater in East Troy, Wisconsin. Robert is proudly holding a Custom Shop version of this guitar — the original inspiration for this Artist Series model.

American Special Series Strat-o-Sonic® - This model was originally conceived by Dan Smith, but was "looked at" and reviewed by many others as well. We all felt good about the creative solutioning that drove this instrument — and ultimately, so did all the folks that bought them!

Although based on the traditional Fender® Stratocaster® design, this model was unique. The Strat-o-Sonic guitar had traditional elements of the Stratocaster at its foundation, but with a bevy of distinctive features that truly set the model apart. The guitar featured a body made of Honduran Mahogany with five tone chambers. It was relatively light weight and very resonant. Built in the U.S. factory, it also had a shorter 24 ¾" scale length and used the new Fender Tech-Tonic bridge, allowing for perfectly adjustable intonation string by string. It was available with your choice of Fender Atomic II humbucking pickups or Fender Black Dove™ P-90 style single-coil pickups. It came in 3 colors. They were Brown Sunburst (shown here), Butterscotch Blonde, (shown here) and Crimson Transparent.

Although initially embraced by the playing community, the model was ultimately discontinued in 2007. It is now difficult to find one of these models used despite the fact that a fair number were sold, so it appears that buyers have held onto these guitars.

American Series Telecaster® HH/HS - In January of 2003, Fender® introduced two new versions of the American Standard Telecaster. The Telecaster has stood the test of time and still hangs out right at the top of the heap when it comes to "twangy" single-coil pickup sound.

The first single coils were made in the 1920s by George Beauchamp and Adolph Rickenbacker, who refined their design into the external magnet "horseshoe pickup," patented in 1937. Gibson was also producing single coils in the '30s for Hawaiian guitars, most notably their "bar pickups" in 1935. But it was Fender's design, featuring a coil wound around magnetic slugs, that ultimately set the standard. Simply stated: *nothing* sounds like a Tele.

But ... how about a Telecaster that feels like a Tele and yet sounds like a Les Paul? The American Telecaster HH was just such a beast. The Tele® HH was equipped with two of our Atomic II humbuckers and delivered a thicker, fuller sound than its single-coil predecessor.

Who hasn't said that Keith Richards' rhythm tone is pretty wonderful? Like, no one, right? For decades he's used his modified Telecasters — each typically with an added humbucker in the neck position — to great effect for both stage and studio. The American Telecaster Series HS offers that same configuration; namely, the perfect combination of thick, rich humbucking tones paired with the bite of Fender's iconic single-coil treble pickup mounted on a steel plate. The Telecaster HS employs one Atomic II humbucker and one American Series Tele single-coil pickup.

These guitars were available in Black, Chrome Blue, Chrome Red and Pewter. Later, because of consumer demand, a 3-ply pickguard was added to this model. That said, the instruments pictured here capture how they originally appeared when introduced in January 2003. After the S-1™ switch was introduced later in 2003, it was subsequently added to this model and marketed as an upgraded version. The S-1 performed a variety of different functions depending on the specific model in question. In this particular instance, it offered series/parallel options in the middle position.

American Highway One™ Series Stratocaster® -
The Highway One™ Series Stratocaster was the brainchild of both Richard McDonald (at the time, my own boss and marketing manager for Fender® Electric Guitars & Basses) and Dan Smith (Senior VP of R & D).
Although the American Series Stratocaster was still one of the most popular selling Stratocaster models, consumers seemed to be torn between the quality of the Ensenada-built Standard Strat® and the American Standard Strat built in Corona, CA. The idea behind Highway One was to essentially create an American made Stratocaster that was as basic as an American made guitar could be. "Everything you need, and nothing you don't need" was how Richard McDonald described the guitar at the time.

The few things that made this guitar different from the American Standard Strat were simple. The Highway One came with either a rosewood or maple fingerboard. It featured three alnico magnet, staggered pole piece single-coil pickups. It used the standard Fender synchronized tremolo (as opposed to the American Standard which used the 2-point synchronized tremolo), and it came in a gig bag as opposed to a hardshell case.

The finish at the time of introduction was gloss satin lacquer, although this changed later. The Highway One Series expanded to include Telecaster, P Bass and J Bass models. The available colors were Sapphire Blue Transparent, Crimson Red Transparent, Cocoa Transparent, Teal Green Transparent, and Honey Blonde Transparent (shown here).

American Highway One™ Series Stratocaster® HSS & Telecaster® – As the Highway One™ Series took shape, we looked to one obvious source for inspiration: Fender guitars that had been played long and hard in clubs and on the road. What were the most common modifications that workhorse instruments underwent (many times by the hands that played them)? If you lived through the '60s and '70s and played guitar, you pretty much HAD to have stripped the finish off of a Fender guitar at one point or another! It was undeniably tempting. The practice of removing a battered finish and replacing it with a new coat of lacquer was all too common, and all too often done by the instrument's owner. The Highway One HSS Stratocaster sports one of the most common aftermarket looks: the see-though stained finish. The other common aftermarket mod done to a Strat® was to replace the treble pickup with a humbucker for solos. Add a 22nd fret, and you're off to the races! The Highway One used the then new "Atomic II" humbucker. The available colors for the Highway One Strat HSS were, Cocoa Transparent, Walnut & Amber (shown here).

The Highway One Telecaster featured a different set of see-through low gloss, satin lacquer finishes: 3-color Sunburst, Daphne Blue Transparent, Crimson Red Transparent, & Honey Blonde Transparent (shown here). Throughout the development of the Highway One Series, finishes changed from acrylic lacquer to satin lacquer. The Highway One Series Telecaster came equipped with two Hot Tele® single-coil pickups with alnico 3 magnets (neck & bridge). They were new pickups at the time and many thought they rivaled the American Standard Tele pickups. The guitar was also equipped with a vintage style 3 saddle bridge with brass saddles.

American Highway One™ Series Showmaster® HSS & Toronado® - As the Highway One™ Series evolved, two more of Fender's original body designs followed suit in the new American Highway One Series.

The Showmaster® (basically a Custom Shop body design) came with a 24-fret neck and an original Floyd Rose® tremolo with matching chrome hardware. The pickups used on this model were two Fender® Standard Strat® single coils and 1 Fender Enforcer Humbucking pickup, with 5-way switching, a single volume and tone knob. This Showmaster model was also offered in an HH version. (not shown)

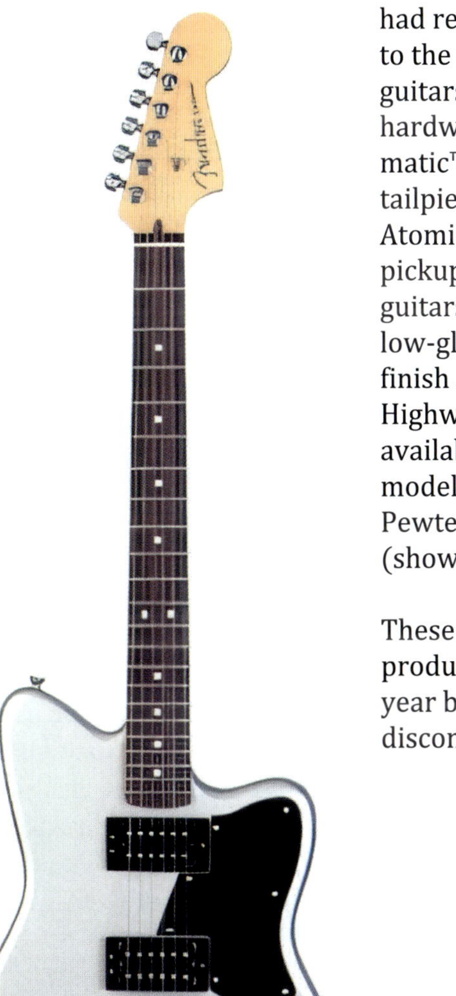

The Toronado®, which had recently been added to the Corona lineup of guitars. had chrome hardware, an Adjust-o-matic™ bridge with stop tailpiece, and two Fender Atomic II humbucking pickups. Both of these guitars featured the same low-gloss, satin lacquer finish as the other Highway One guitars. The available colors for these models were Black, Pewter, and Chrome Silver (shown here).

These two models were produced for roughly a year before they were discontinued.

Deluxe Series Acoustasonic® - The Acoustasonic was another very innovative design that took the previous "Stratacoustic®" to an entirely different level. The thought behind this guitar was one of creating a true Stratocaster®, making the look and feel of an electric, but having it sound like an acoustic — basically bridging the gap between electric and acoustic guitar players. The target player for this guitar was the acoustic player interested in electric guitar, as well as the electric player interested in acoustic guitar. Many people who owned a Stratocaster bought this guitar, using it live and in the studio as well.

This idea was primarily Dan Smith's and he worked with outside sources to bring the concept to fruition. While this instrument did not gain the popularity that we had hoped, it did prove once again that Fender® was and is one of the most creative and innovative guitar companies in the world.

This guitar consisted of a totally hollowed-out Stratocaster alder body with a directional woodgrain-like pattern on the graphite composite top. While a Stratocaster body thickness is 1.75 inches in depth, this Acoustasonic Strat® body was just slightly deeper, at just over 2 inches in depth. The composite top sounds like spruce but is much lighter and stronger. What looks like bridge mounting posts are actually the volume and tone controls. This electric/acoustic guitar's super lightweight design used active electronics with a 3-piece piezo under the bridge pickup system. This traditional electric guitar neck was perfect for the electric guitarist wanting a Stratocaster that plays like "Old Faithful" but sounds like an acoustic. An amazing, innovative instrument.

A Fender® deluxe gig bag was included. Color options were Ebony Transparent, Crimson Transparent, Pewter & Sapphire Blue Transparent (shown here).

Special Edition Esquire & Showmaster® Scorpion, Celtic - In 2002 we began the process of working with the Cort Korea factory in the manufacturing of Fender® branded instruments. There was no question that Fender Japan had the ability to produce top quality Fender guitars, but Korean factories had also gained the knowledge and technology needed to produce top caliber instruments as well.

A trip to the Cort factory in Korea confirmed my beliefs that the factory was up for the challenge. It was time to work with these factories on new Fender ideas.

While the Fender Scorpion Esquire & Celtic Showmaster were an extension of traditional Fender designs, these models featured set-in, bound necks. The super-slim contoured mahogany body (Esquire) or Basswood body (Showmaster) featured Black high-gloss and matte Silver finishes, respectively. Both were powered with a single Fender Atomic II humbucking pickup and controlled via a single volume knob.

The "theme" of the 12-fret inlays on these was derived from Celtic mythology, which includes scorpions and designs with a hint of Irish tradition woven in. In addition, our offices were based in Arizona, where many of us lived — scorpions were a common sight.

Introduced in January of 2003, these guitars definitely sparked interest, sold well and showed the world what Korean factories could do. These guitars were relatively short-lived but also included (not shown here): the Esquire Custom GT with racing stripe, Showmaster Celtic H, Showmaster Scorpion HH and Showmaster H w/trem. The single "H" naturally implied one pickup, while "HH" implied two.

Special Edition Custom Telecaster® HH FMT - The Special Edition Custom Telecaster HH FMT was an affordable, versatile revamp of Fender's most popular cornerstone guitar.

This guitar was part of the new series of "Special Edition Set-Neck" guitars that was introduced in January of 2003. It featured a carved flamed maple top over a mahogany body. These were set-neck instruments and this Tele® had crème neck & body binding. It had smoked chrome hardware and a string-through body bridge. At the time this was released, we used our Fender Atomic II humbucker in the bridge position and our Fender Black Canyon humbucker in the neck position. The pickups were splitable by way of the push-pull tone knob. This model came in Black Cherry Sunburst and Amber (shown here).

For the longest time, the general rule of thumb was that if a guitar that was imported from overseas, the Seymour Duncan-supplied pickups Fender® used in their guitars were typically "Duncan Designed" pickups. These pickups were created by the Seymour Duncan company based on existing designs but manufactured in Korea and sold to Fender to be used on lower-priced guitars.

Obviously, Seymour Duncan's relationship with Fender was extremely strong and we proudly used their pickups throughout our catalog for many years. With the Special Edition Custom Telecaster our goal was to put American made Seymour Duncan pickups in this new, offshore, cutting-edge Fender model. A year later we accomplished that goal by adding a Pearly Gates™ Plus pickup in the bridge position and a '59 Model™, reverse polarity humbucker in the neck position.

The Pearly Gates Plus and '59 RP models were conceived during Mike Lewis' tenure as Marketing Manager. The Pearly Gates Plus had made its way into the Lone Star Strat® and the addition of the '59 RP came with the Big Apple Strat. These two humbucking pickups were designed by Seymour Duncan for Fender and were used in a fair number of the double-humbucker guitars during my tenure. The unique and highly usable 3-way switch wiring was conceived by noted Fender electronics guru Michael Frank Braun.

This set the tone for strategic placement of American made Seymour Duncan pickups in all of our upcoming Korean imported models. This model proved to be incredibly successful and has withstood the test of time, remaining in the Fender assortment to this day.

Standard Series Satin Stratocaster® - The number one best selling guitar for Fender had been our Standard Stratocaster made in our Ensenada, Mexico factory for years. Because of the ongoing popularity of the Standard Strat®, it seemed fitting to increase the options of this model for the consumer.

This was simply a cosmetic variation to our Standard Strat assortment at the time. The features were identical on these models to those on the Standard Strat, with the visual additions being a 3-ply B/W/B pickguard, a black tremolo arm tip and a black switch tip. The satin finishes available were Midnight Blue, Midnight Wine, Candy Apple Red (shown here) and Gun Metal Blue (shown here). This model was discontinued in 2007.

When Fender® built its factory in Ensenada Mexico, it opened the door for North American Fender production in an area other than southern California. Because of the close proximity of Fender's R & D department in Corona, Ca., overseeing the quality and standards of Fender instruments was easily regulated and Fender models could be produced more affordably. Because of this, the Standard Strat as we know it today is still manufactured in Mexico along with many other very popular Fender models.

Artist Series Marcus Miller Jazz Bass® - One of the most accomplished bass players of all time, Marcus Miller has always been closely associated with the Fender® Jazz Bass. Marcus is a composer, producer, arranger and multi-instrumentalist most well-known for playing with legends like Miles Davis, David Sanborn, Herbie Hancock, Eric Clapton and Luther Vandross. His stint as musical director and bassist for the *Saturday Night Live* band was a personal favorite.

The 4-string version of his Jazz Bass initially came out in 1998 and was manufactured in Japan; but in 2003 we released this beautiful 5-string American made version.

The look of this bass is a beautiful homage to the Fender '70s Jazz Bass with its big pearl block inlays, maple fingerboard, and ash body. This bass is truly unique due to the finer details: small variations on everything from the pickguard to the knob spacing, the ash tray cover, the specially-designed string trees and the many additional minor "deviations," so to speak.

The Artist Series Marcus Miller Jazz Bass also uses an active/passive switch, which has become requested more and more by professional bass players over the years. The switch engages the active preamp when in the "on" position for a silent "hum free" signal, but when in the "off" position, the bass is essentially a normal passive electric bass.

American Highway One™ Series Precision & Jazz Bass®

- With the launch and success of the new Highway One™ Series of guitars in 2002 it was a given that we needed to include the Precision Bass® and Jazz Bass® as well. In keeping with the mantra of the Highway One Series, the idea here was to manufacture American made instruments that would slide into the price list just below the current American Standard instruments. An attractive price point, but one that still allowed us to retain many of the more expensive features of the American Standard.

In terms of Fender basses, the standard specifications for neck shapes & profiles, nut width, frets and fingerboards are as follows: maple, modern C-Shape, with a rosewood or maple fingerboard with 21 medium jumbo frets. Standard Fender bass nut widths in most cases are 1.5" for a Jazz Bass 4-string, and 1.5" for a Precision Bass. Meanwhile, both 5-string Precision and Jazz basses feature a 1.875" nut width.

At the time of release, the Highway One Precision Bass & Jazz Bass used the same pickups as our Mexico Standard Series basses. The success of the series would warrant future upgrades to the Highway One Series of guitars and basses, including pickups and hardware.

The same colors available on the Standard Series Highway One Stratocaster and Telecaster were also applied on the Precision Bass and Jazz Bass. These basses were available in 3-color Sunburst (shown here), Daphne Blue Transparent, Crimson Red Transparent and Honey Blonde Transparent (shown here). and Crimson Red Transparent.

Classic Series '51 P Bass® - Although the first Audiovox® electric basses were made by Seattle builder Paul Tutmarc in the 1930s, Fender's '51 P Bass was the electric bass that really got everyone's attention. Cosmetically the model is the perfect match to the Broadcaster and Telecaster with its black pickguard, maple neck and butterscotch finish. Many collectors have referred to the early Precision Bass as the "Telecaster Bass" due to the narrow "Tele-like" headstock and matching appointments.

The upright violin bass had already been long established as the percussive lower-register note accompaniment to the drummer in the performance and recording of popular music. Big bands, jazz combos, piano trios, all relied on the warm low-end throb of the upright bass. The bass player's curse, however, was hauling the large instrument around from gig to gig — no small feat.

Being heard became a new challenge in the early '50s with the introduction of the electric guitar into swing, rock, country and jazz ensembles. As the music itself trended toward higher volume levels, it wasn't uncommon to quite simply overpower the acoustic bass. Leo Fender had had many requests from bassists in well-known touring bands that visited the factory to develop an electric bass that matched the output of his guitars; and the idea was born.

The early Precision Bass has a single-coil pickup very akin to the Telecaster pickup; sonically, it was an instant success. Stages and studios alike immediately embraced the punch, clarity and versatility of the Precision Bass.

This reissue bass, manufactured in the Fender® Japan factory, has an ash body, maple neck and came in Butterscotch Blonde just like it did in 1951.

Deluxe Series Aerodyne™ Jazz Bass® - The Aerodyne (an aviation reference essentially referring to an "aerodynamic" aircraft) was a new and welcome addition to the Fender® assortment of basses sold in the US. Fender of Japan had initially concocted this great idea — essentially a variant of the Jazz Bass with a decidedly unique cosmetic vibe — and had produced them with success in the Japanese market.

Naturally, to be considered for inclusion in the US domestic offering, any idea or design had to be reviewed and approved by us. Timing is everything, as they say, and you simply can't have a domestic model competing with a foreign made instrument with similar features and price point. To that end, Japan had been making this bass and we liked it but were not realistically able to introduce it domestically until 2003.

What made this bass different from our traditional Jazz Bass was the fact that it had a carved basswood body and bound top with no pickguard. The single-bound top was striking against the black finish, and access to the controls was via routing from the rear, so a pickguard was not necessary. The input jack quickly became a standard recessed "Stratocaster®" style jack but pictured here is the instrument that was released initially. The P/J pickup combination did not leverage the same pickups used in Japan's P Bass and J Bass; those were "vintage wound" pickups. These were purpose-built for this model and were wound slightly hotter. With the smoked chrome hardware and matching headstock, this bass has a very sleek look. Though still remaining in the Fender lineup at this time, the model has continued to evolve quite a bit.

Nashville: July 2003

Artist Series Mark Knopfler Stratocaster® - Although this guitar actually came out in May of 2003, it wasn't officially on the pricelist until July and was given its true introduction at the Nashville 2003 NAMM Show. The development of this model came from our Fender® design team in Europe.

Europe, and in particular the United Kingdom, has certainly introduced its fair share of astonishing guitarists to the world. Few guitar players of any era have had the impact that Mark Knopfler managed to achieve in 1977 with Dire Straits' "Sultans of Swing". Talk about an absolute sonic homage to the Stratocaster ... wow! Knopfler's playing and note choice throughout the song is nothing short of dazzling, and the tune has stood the test of time as an absolute classic.

Mark has played a Stratocaster from the beginning, and many of Dire Straits' biggest hits feature the unmistakable "fingerpicked Strat" sound that fans worldwide have come to know and love. Fender felt it was time to pay tribute the best way we knew how: with a new signature model based on Mark's exacting specifications.

This guitar came exactly the way Mark liked it and is based on his own modified Stratocaster. The model featured a '57-style ash body, with a '62 common "C" shaped neck and rosewood fingerboard with medium jumbo frets. The neck sports a 7.25" radius, as typically found on older Fender guitars up to the early 1980s (prior to our introduction of the flatter, modern 9.5-inch radius). The guitar utilized three Texas Special single-coil pickups and came in Knopfler's favorite color: Hot Rod Red.

Artist Series Jag-Stang® - The impact that Kurt Cobain and Nirvana had on music in the '80s essentially changed the face of rock-'n'-roll. Kurt was a complete original, and his guitar was no different.

The Jag-Stang basically took design elements from the Fender® Mustang® and Jaguar® (both were guitars that Kurt played), and then "melted" them together to hatch this unique design. Originally Kurt supplied Fender with a pieced-together Polaroid photo (shown on the following page)), stating that he wanted the body to look something like this picture. This body shape was a first for Fender, and the original model was built for Kurt in the Fender Custom Shop.

After Kurt worked closely with Larry Brooks (Custom Shop builder) putting together the specs on this new Fender design, Larry built the first prototype for Kurt. Nirvana was on tour at that time, so Larry shipped it to him. There are very few pictures of Kurt playing that Custom Shop guitar on the *In Utero* tour, but Kurt *did* play it, wrote notes on it with a sharpie, and then sent it back to Larry. The original intent was to release Kurt's new Fender model in 1994, but because of his untimely passing, the release of his model was put on hold.

This Artist Series Jag-Stang was originally released in 1996 after being on hold for 2 years, as a production model manufactured in the Japan factory. Because the body shape was different than anything we had tooling for in the U.S. and because it was an instrument that was already being manufactured in the Fender® Japan factory, it became something I could easily bring into the US market. And I did so in 2003.

My approach and thought on this model, was to bring attention to the fact that Kurt was a Fender guy, and to remind people that roughly 10 years prior, Kurt was working on a model, *his* model ... and that his model had been planned for release. I did have to obtain permission from Kurt's widow to effectively re-release the model. It wasn't easy, but we got it done. Although the re-release wasn't shown in print until January 2004 in our *Fender Frontline* catalog, the guitar was officially available in November 2003.

The Artist Series Jag-Stang was made in Japan and came in Fiesta Red and Sonic Blue, with a rosewood fingerboard. The production Jag-Stang included a "vintage style" single-coil pickup in the neck position and one "Dragster" humbucker in the bridge position, each with its own toggle switch that can be used to switch from on-off-or out of phase settings. The guitar employs the Mustang's "Dynamic Vibrato" bridge and has a short scale 24-inch scale length neck.

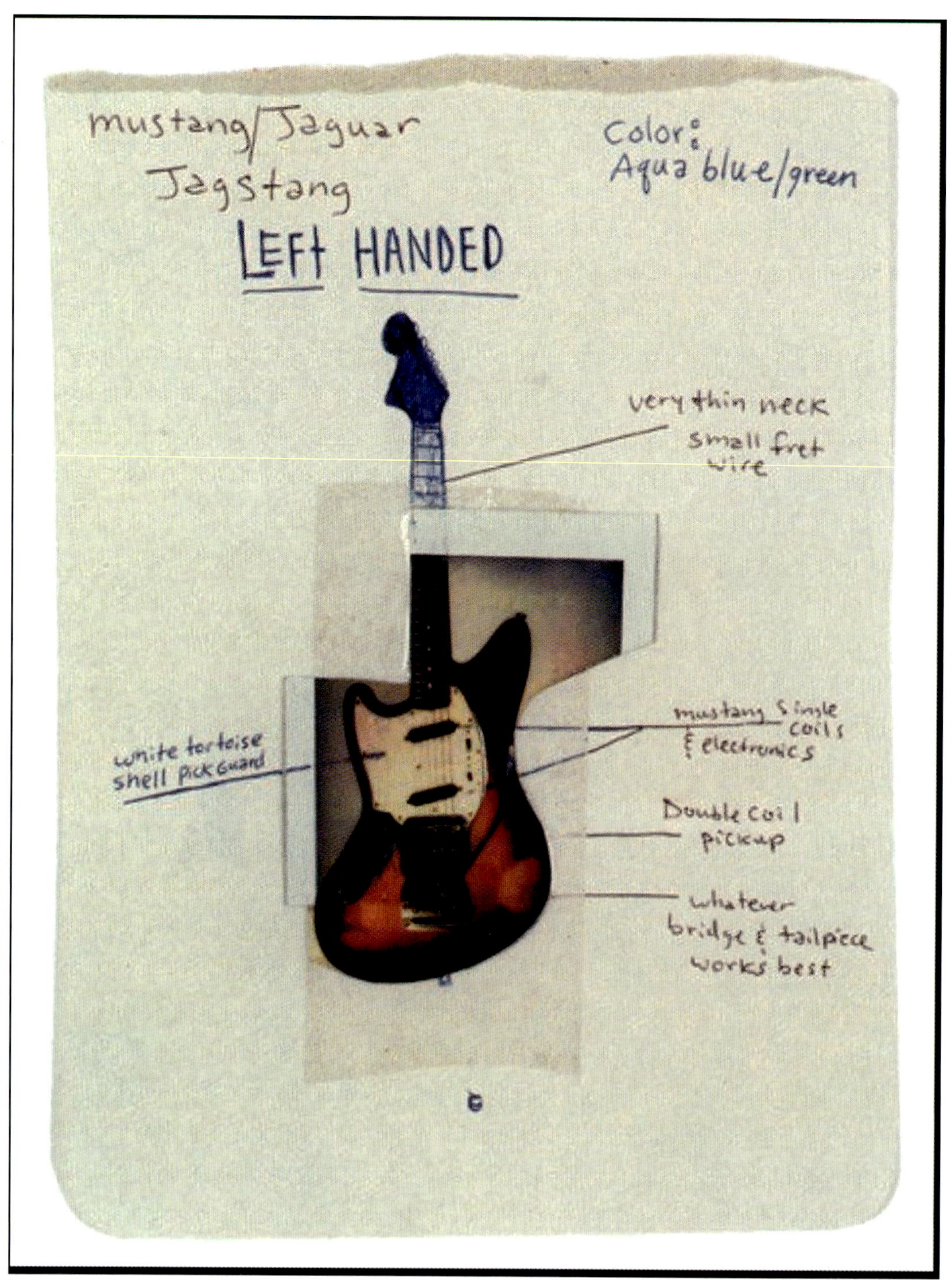

The above is a copy of the original pieced-together Polaroid that Kurt Cobain assembled for the Custom Shop's Larry Brooks and our R & D team to assist in designing his signature model.

American Series W/ S-1™ Switch - The revamp of the American Series Stratocaster® with single-coil pickups was subtle, but the implementation of the new S-1™ switch on guitars with humbucking pickups brought the offering to a new level. Although we were already working on the upcoming new American Deluxe Series at this time, our goal was to begin producing S-1™ switching in American Series models with humbuckers as a means of providing players with more tonal options for the Stratocaster. We introduced these guitars in July in Nashville.

When Bill Carson visited the Fender® booth in Nashville in the summer of 2003, all of us in the Fender family were (of course!) excited to see him. He was 77 at the time but lived in Nashville, so it was an easy drive downtown to visit us at NAMM. Of course, Bill's fiery personality, humor and wit had not aged a bit and we loved sharing any time with Bill we could.

I was demonstrating a blue American Standard Strat® HH while Bill watched. I engaged the S-1™ switch, put the 5-way switch in the middle position, and played. "I'll be damned!" he exclaimed. I had a traditional two single-coil "out of phase" sound coming out of a Stratocaster with two humbucking pickups. The guitar sounded not at all the way a traditional humbucking pickup should sound. People did not know that we were already working on the upcoming new American Deluxe Series at this time, and S-1™ switching was going to be featured throughout this new upcoming series. By introducing the switch into the current American Standard Strat, we managed to create a lot of excitement.

In terms of the switch itself, *nothing* had been done like this before and it was and still is an exciting Fender innovation. Many of us have modified our guitars as a means of enabling additional sounds out of our pickups. And, frequently, we accomplished that by modifying our guitars with mini toggle switches of all kinds. Not only was the instrument look altered, but frequently additional drillholes (at a bare minimum, in the pickguard) were required.

The S-1™ switch was simply a push-push switch housed within the crown of the volume knob. You couldn't see it if you didn't know it was there. It just looks like (and also functions as) a standard volume knob. Not only that, but the switch served a variety of different functions dependent on model and context: splitting coils, switching pickups in and out of phase, etc. The following diagrams (on the next page) explain it all very well.

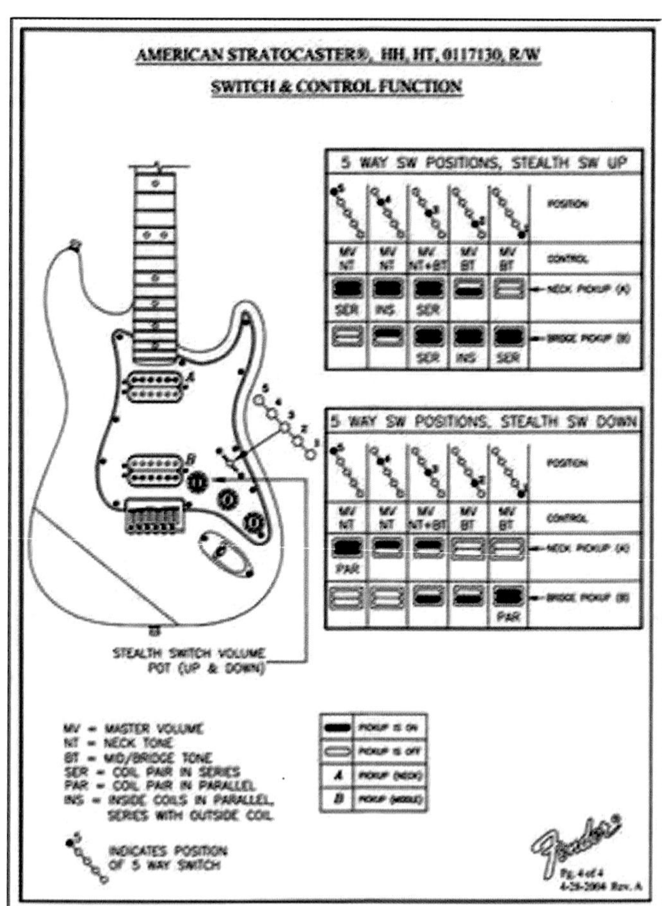

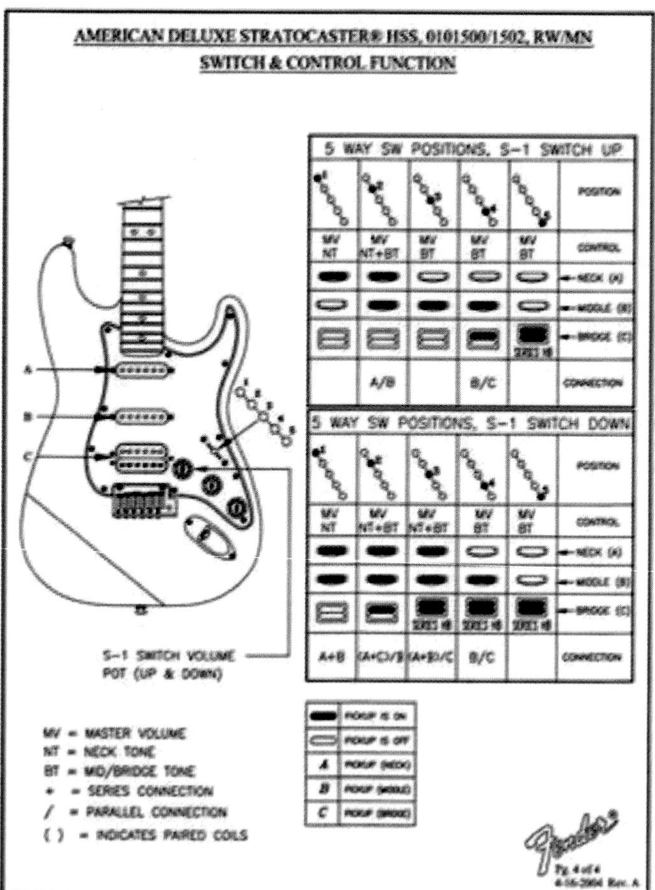

The HH hardtail American Series Stratocaster came with one Black Cobra™ (bridge) humbucker and one Sidewinder™ (neck) humbucker. This model came with a rosewood fingerboard.
The HSS version came with 1 Diamondback (bridge) humbucker and two Tex- Mex single coils. It as well as the other two models came with either a rosewood or maple fingerboard. The three single-coil version of this model had three Tex Mex single-coil pickups in it. The available colors for these these four versions were: Chrome Red, Chrome Blue, Chrome Silver and Butterscotch Blonde.

More on the new S-1™- It is not often that innovative new functionality of this nature is introduced to the electric guitar platform. Floyd Rose® certainly did it, along with a few others, but the basic concept of a great invention that holds its own over years is a rare thing; and this rings true with so many things we did at Fender®. The S-1 switch is a prime example.
While the functionality itself has been covered above, other "things" are of note regarding this switch. Originally the name I shopped around for the switch was "Stealth," for obvious reasons. However, when securing names for basically anything these days, there is always a legal process that has to be executed in order to secure a name. These legal terms are simple: Registered Trademark (™), Registered Copyright (®), etc. You see them throughout this book and everywhere else.
As for the term "Stealth", it just so happens that Fender is not *quite* as influential as our U.S. government who of course had used the term for the F-117A Stealth Fighter and B-2 Stealth Bomber. We unfortunately could not use what was to me, the most obvious name. After many ideas and much research, I finally suggested that we keep it simple, and the name "S-1™" was decided and then trademarked by our legal counsel. We were working on and finalizing different volume knobs (S-1 switches) for use with the new American Deluxe Series, adding many useable tonal variations on Strat®, Tele®, P Bass® and Jazz Bass® models. The switch is also still used on Custom Shop instruments as well.

American Series Telecaster® Ash - When we think of a Fender® electric guitar, of course the Telecaster® is one of the models that most frequently to immediately spring to mind. At least that's true for many of we guitar players, anyway. The instrument here was intended as the purest modern-day take on the Tele that we could deliver.

The Tele actually started life as the Broadcaster; and we know that for a brief period in 1951 the model was released with no name at all — these instruments are affectionately referred to as the "Nocaster" guitars. The reason for the name disappearance was that Leo Fender was in need of a new name for the Broadcaster, after the Gretsch Drum company had taken legal action, claiming that the name was too close to that of their own Broadkaster drum kit. So, the Telecaster platform had been a work in process, so to speak, from 1949. Its almost-finalized "take" came into being in the fall of 1950, which really marked the widely-embraced inception of the Fender electric guitar. THIS started it.

Why, then, did Leo ultimately decide on the name "Telecaster" shortly thereafter? The "future" was where the inventive mind of Leo was always focused. At that time black and white television was the latest technical breakthrough. The Telecaster name was invented as a nod to this, and Leo quickly pressed the "go" button. The 1952 Telecaster was officially created.

It was that original body shape, neck, and headstock shape that started it all.

So - back to 2003. At the time, we didn't really have what we would call "today's" version of the original 1952 Telecaster. We had the American Vintage reissue, which was true and accurate to the specs of the original. For this version, a very similar approach and way of thinking was applied as that had driven the creation of the 2004 50th Anniversary 1954 Stratocaster (which we'll cover later). This guitar featured an ash body, Butterscotch Blonde finish, single-ply pickguard, and a 9.5" radius, one-piece maple, modern C-shape neck. Other features such as bridge and tuners were the same as the American Standard Telecaster at the time. We did add a steel bridge plate to the bridge, for added sustain and richer tone. This model was our solution to the "modern day" Telecaster.

Deluxe Series Cyclone® HH - While we had introduced the Cyclone II in the summer of 2002, as previously shown, it was different, with Jaguar® pickups and switching.

This new model satisfied the needs of the player that appreciated the guitar's unique aesthetics but preferred humbucking pickups. It instantly opened up the Cyclone world to a new audience of players. The body shape, in general, was a creative and original Fender® iconic design and this opened up a new doorway for players.

We not only offered it in an HH configuration with Atomic II humbucking pickups, but we also offered it in a HS config making that humbucker/single-coil combination available in the Cyclone model for the first time. The HS model used the same Atomic II humbucker (W/B) bobbin (bridge) and a Tex-Mex single-coil (neck). The guitar's electronics were simple. Two pickups with a 3-way switch. The maple neck had a 24¾" scale length, a 9.5" radius, and a rosewood fingerboard. The neck shape was a modern C-shape. The hardware was our standard chrome hardware. This guitar was made in our Mexico factory like its brother, the Cyclone II.

This model was available in Daphne Blue, Pewter, Orange and Black (shown here) and came in a standard gig bag. The Cyclone Series lasted for almost 10 years but was discontinued in 2007.

Limited Edition Series Splatter Stratocaster® - One of the things I loved the most about my job at Fender® was that it offered me the freedom to get creative. The aim was to try to get into the mind of a customer, think about what might be appealing, and then figure out a way to create it. Awareness of what was happening in the market and the world was always critical. Incoming phone calls from all kinds of players were a constant "force," and each conversation presented a creative fact-finding opportunity.

Rarely could one create something that universally appealed to everyone, but if it hadn't been done before and if our collective group liked it, I was given the green light.

I knew I was onto something when I showed Bill Schultz (Fender owner and CEO) the first sample of the Splatter Stratocaster, and he asked me to leave it in his office. It was different enough that it inspired interest on his part, and that was good enough for me.

I spent a week at our Fender Ensenada factory and we had a blast experimenting with different colors and techniques. A simple "spin art" painting technique was used in this process and we spun the bodies at different speeds, dropping the paint onto the bodies at different intervals creating a unique result on every guitar. It took some thought because ultimately, we had to (and did) figure out how to attach the pickguard so that the artwork would all remain cohesive on the final assembled instrument.

This process was somewhat labor intensive, but we were still able to keep costs reasonable. While this guitar was first shown in July of 2003, production was limited to roughly 700 guitars available to the global market. Basically, each one of these standard Stratocasters was unique and "one of a kind" because of the painting technique used in the process.

The result? Certainly not for everyone but appealing to a large crowd from classic Fender collectors to general guitar enthusiasts. This guitar was of course a Limited Edition in that we only produced it for a short period of time. These are quite hard to find used these days. I was told by a friend of mine at Fender at the NAMM Show a few years back, that people still ask Fender if they will ever make these again. Perhaps they will?

Anaheim: January 2004

The 50th Anniversary of the Stratocaster®

Custom Shop 50th Anniversary Stratocaster -

Although the Custom Shop and what it produced was not my charge, I was asked to help provide any input I could to the '54 Custom Shop model. When we sat down in 2003 to discuss what we would do to commemorate this anniversary, I had my plan already together for what I envisioned in terms of factory production line instruments for this project, and I was excited. This opportunity would only come once in my lifetime.

As we talked, I happened to ask about what the Custom Shop was planning to do. The response: crickets chirping as folks looked at each other. It was clear that *that* particular piece of the puzzle had not yet been discussed. A phone call to Mike Eldred (Custom Shop Marketing Manager at that time) was made right away and HIS plan was hatched.

The Custom Shop had previously released various versions of the '54 Stratocaster. Mike & Dan Smith had a good relationship with Richard Smith, author of *The Sound Heard 'Round the World* and owner of serial #0100, one of the original 1954 Stratocaster guitars. Richard's guitar was used to model this recreation and Mike Eldred spearheaded this project for the Custom Shop, duplicating the instrument and securing Richard Smith's famous original '54 Strat® in the history books forever.

I had opened my mouth and asked the question. Now I had a great deal of work to do on not only the Custom Shop model, but the standard production line models as well.

One of the biggest challenges for this project was the fact that we didn't have the original tooling to make the knobs. As I quickly learned, the knob size was different on the original '54 as you can see in the picture here. Bigger in diameter. Another question that needed to be answered: since plastic as we knew it back then was evolving, what exactly were the plastic parts made of? This meant I needed to go find original plastic parts. Knobs, pickguard material and pickup covers. Not an easy task. After much exploring, I finally located these parts and purchased them, at outrageous prices. It simply had to be done to recreate this masterpiece.

During the months of work on this project, the public certainly anticipated what was coming in 2004 in the way of the 50th anniversary of this icon. That said, the sheer amount of phone calls I received on the topic reached a point of requiring active filtering, and that was done by Rose Bishop — my dear friend and assistant who really protected some of us who were constantly being bombarded on the front lines. The excitement itself, of course, was always appreciated and frequently insightful. The job was to "listen".

I ended up speaking with a gentleman from Texas named John Andrews. John owned an original 1954. He emailed me a photograph. It looked very similar to Richard Smith's guitar — but what I particularly noticed was that the photo was of the guitar in the original case with the original strap. Just as it had come in 1954.
Those two pieces were what we needed. John sent me the case with the strap in it. I sent the strap to Levy's (in Canada) who were famous for their strap prowess, to have them recreate it; which they did with no problems.

The one common thread that these three models (as well as the Golden 50th Anniversary model that would come out in July) had, was that a total of 1,954 of these models were ever to be made, and we kept to that promise.

All of the Custom Shop versions were Masterbuilt. The instrument came with the certificate signed by the builder himself. Those guys were John Cruz, Chris Fleming, Dennis Galuszka, Greg Fessler, and the late John English.

The model featured a light Ash body (less than 8 lbs.), a 2-Tone Sunburst nitrocellulose lacquer Finish, a one-piece maple neck and fingerboard, and a 1954 "U" neck shape. The fingerboard radius was the classic old-school 7.25" with a 25.5" scale length. The width at nut was 1.650" and the neck had 21 vintage-style frets. One of the most important achievements was that we created three New 1954 single-coil Strat® pickups hand-wound by Abigail Ybarra. She was still at Fender and was in fact the very person who had hand-wound these pickups back in 1954. The hardware was nickel/chrome, the controls were the standard 1 volume, 2 tone, with 3-way switching (not 5-way) and the tuners were also vintage style. The bridge was an American Vintage Synchronized Tremolo with bridge cover, and the pickguard was 3-Ply Parchment. The guitar came in a vintage style brown 1954 case made by G & G cases.

When all was said and done, the result was a spot-on reproduction of Richard Smith's original, with a "Closet Classic" finish (meaning: weather-checked, but not "beat up"). This guitar was featured on the cover of *Vintage Guitar* magazine in November of 2004, and an interview with Mike Eldred and myself were included in that magazine.

American Deluxe Series 50th Anniversary Stratocaster® - In 2004, we launched the new American Deluxe Series of guitars and basses as you are about to see in the following pages. This 50th Anniversary Stratocaster guitar was based on this new design, and to commemorate the 50th anniversary, we made this model.

At the time, I had not really considered doing this model, but Rich Siegle (Director of Branding at Fender) repeatedly encouraged the idea. Rich had been at Fender for quite a while before I had come onboard. He was/is a great marketing guy, not to mention an excellent guitar player. Rich has a charismatic personality onstage, yet was typically a fairly quiet guy at work. This model really required thought and planning, but Rich was a strong supporter every step of the way.

The instrument featured all of the new attributes of the American Deluxe Series guitars. This model had an alder, 2-tone sunburst body, but added gold hardware and the 50th anniversary logo inscribed on the pickguard as well as the gold 50th anniversary neckplate. This guitar also came with the new S-1™ switching and the new SCN pickups (to be covered later) incorporated into it as well. It included a vintage tweed case. 1,954 guitars were made.

American Series 50th Anniversary Stratocaster® - In 2003, we began the process of discussing what we would do for the upcoming year. 2004 meant that we would be celebrating the 50th anniversary of the most famous electric guitar ever invented, and this project was my "baby," so to speak. I remember Ritchie Fliegler (who hired me) looking at me and saying, in so many words, "This is your ass on the line." We would only get one chance at this, and it would be one of the biggest projects I had done up to this point. There was no margin for error. It had to be right.

This American Series guitar was basically today's American version of the original. Meaning, if we had taken the subtle improvements that have been made over the previous 50 years up until that time and produced the modern take on the Stratocaster that was conceived in 1954, it would be this guitar. The body is Ash with a 2-tone sunburst finish, just like its grandfather had. It was also equipped with Custom Shop 1954 pickups (the same ones used in the Custom Shop 50th Anniversary edition) along with a "Delta Tone" high output bridge pickup and a no-load tone control for the middle and bridge pickups.

While it's a fact that in 1954, some of the production model Stratocaster guitars were made with a non-tremolo (or what came to be called a "hardtail") bridge, the vast majority of those initial Strat guitars did feature a tremolo ... and we kept true to that here. We topped the package off with a special 50th anniversary chrome neck plate and vintage tweed case.

This guitar took all the mojo of the original 1954 Stratocaster and combined it with today's modern accoutrements — a fitting homage to the classic iconic model!

American Deluxe Series Stratocaster® - Although the American Deluxe Series had existed since 1995, we rolled out a major series-wide update in 2004. As we prepared this "re-launch" of the new series of American Deluxe guitars, we made a number of significant upgrades to put these guitars in a class all by themselves. It had been a while since this series had been touched, so we really had to create something special.

The first thing we did was to introduce the new SCN pickups into the series. "SCN" stands for "Samarium Cobalt Noiseless". These pickups were developed by Bill Lawrence and were the result of years of R & D on Bill's part. The challenge was to retain the sound of a single-coil pickup but eliminate that annoying 60-cycle hum. Combining negative & positive polarity and creating a "humbucking" pickup had of course been the solution to that challenge previously. Most folks will agree that the laws of physics are absolute truths. Meaning that, technically, regardless of the appearance of the pickup in question, you essentially needed to make a a humbucking pickup to eliminate that 60-cycle hum. All pickup manufacturers had been doing this for years and attempting to chase the famous Fender single-coil sound. This includes Fender itself, for that matter: consider the Lace Sensor and Vintage Noiseless pickups for example. The point being: these are still fundamentally humbucking pickups.

In meeting with Bill Lawrence and Dan Smith (they had both been colleagues for years), I wanted to know more about Bill, his story and why he felt his new pickup design was right for this undertaking. The famous who, what, where, why, line of questioning. To hear about his history and experience through the decades (Bill certainly wasn't a young man at this point) was exciting, to say the least. In speaking with Bill, I realized that these SCN pickups that he had been working on for the past five years were always targeted specifically for Fender. Bill had not come to us with this new design until this point and time, and that was because he had spent quite literally years dialing in a few versions of nearly perfect classic Fender tone ... and he was ready.

The timing simply worked. The next step was to listen to these pickups. Sound is always subjective, of course. We A/B tested these pickups specifically against American Standard single-coil pickups to compare tone. We did this with numerous sets of single-coil-equipped guitars. Bill's pickups sounded as good as (if not better than) anything we tried. Once Dan Smith, my boss Richard McDonald, myself and few other Fender folks had heard these, we signed off on these pickups and moved forward.

These pickups eliminated the hum. I had truly never heard a "single coil" pickup as quiet as these pickups. I have heard humbuckers that generate more hum than these pickups do! It really is quite amazing.

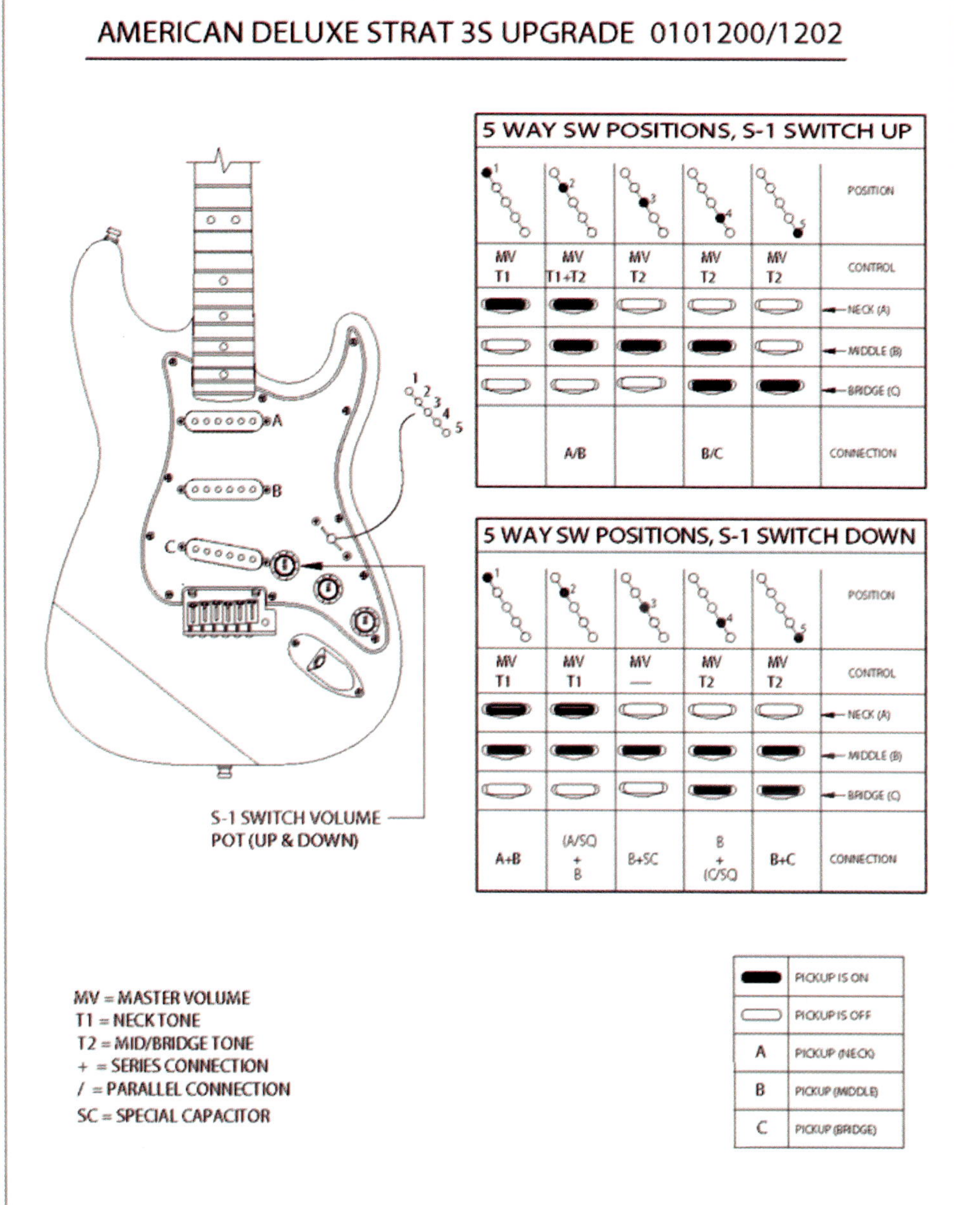

American Deluxe Series using S-1™ Switch - The aim for the series was simple: traditional, classic and yet more cutting edge, while still maintaining the standard Fender® vibe.

We had to create individual PDF diagrams for the instruments with their particular new pickup configurations to best explain exactly what was happening — frankly not only for the consumers to understand what they were hearing, but also for our own staff to be able to effectively explain it. (Additional examples of those diagrams were seen in previous pages.)

Pictured here is the switching diagram for the 3-single coil pickup configuration with the new American Deluxe Series Stratocaster®.

The model was available with either a rosewood or maple fingerboard and came in 3-color Sunburst w/ M/B/M pickguard, Amber w/Brown Shell pickguard, Montego Black w/Gold Vinyl pickguard, Candy Tangerine w/Vintage Shell pickguard, Chrome Silver w/Silver Shell pickguard (shown on previous page). This diagram completed the package and was included in the hardshell case.

American Deluxe Series Stratocaster® HSS LT

- This model was designed to add a few features for the player who, in the old days, might have routed a standard Strat®, installed a bridge position humbucking pickup, and then installed a Floyd Rose® locking tremolo ... all in a quest to get the sounds and performance desired. This was back in the '80s when players like Eddie Van Halen were making the Floyd Rose a mainstay for rock guitarists. Needless to say, modifications this extensive came at the risk of, to some degree, "ruining" the original Strat. And yet, we all knew that risk and did it anyway in the interest of performance!

Although the original Floyd Rose was still available on the Deluxe Stratocaster HSS (made in Mexico), the American-made Stratocaster lineup no longer included the original Floyd Rose as an option.

This new American Deluxe Series model had largely the same features as the new American Deluxe Stratocaster; and most of these new models were available with both rosewood or maple fingerboards (with the exception of ebony fingerboards that were standard on the FMT & QMT models).

The tremolo on this model was a 2-point fulcrum, but the strings locked into the bridge saddles by way of an Allen wrench. The guitar also featured an LSR Roller Nut, to allow zero friction of the strings moving through the nut when the tremolo is used.

These features, along with the locking tuners, truly allowed this guitar to stay in tune when using the tremolo, even to its extreme. The pickups were a Fender DH-1 humbucking pickup in the bridge position, an SC-NLS Strat pickup in the middle, and a Hot SC-NLS Strat pickup in the neck, wound extra hot for balance with the humbucker. This model was offered with either a rosewood or maple fingerboard.

The colors it came in were the new colors and pickguard combinations in this six-model grouping. They were: 3-color Sunburst with M/B/M pickguard, Amber with Brown Shell pickguard, Montego Black with Gold Vinyl pickguard, Candy Tangerine with Vintage Shell pickguard and Chrome Silver with Silver Shell pickguard. These models came in a standard molded hardshell case.

American Deluxe Series Stratocaster® Left-Handed - In most Western countries (like the U.S.) 85 to 90 percent of people are right-handed and 10 to 15 percent of people are left-handed. If you are a left-handed guitarist, then you have undoubtedly always felt a bit discriminated against when it comes to the limited selections of left-handed guitars available. Sometimes it was a real challenge for the left-handed player to really get an instrument precisely to his/her liking. Artists like Hendrix and others had to frequently resort to taking a right-handed instrument and "converting" it for left-handed use.

I worked on this model with a close friend of mine at Fender® who is a lefty and incredibly talented singer, guitarist and composer: Brian Page. Brian always made suggestions to me in terms of models that he felt should be available as a left-handed variant. I learned over time to always ask Brian on every model when we got closer to releasing the new right-handed model. We all agreed that we should offer the new American Deluxe in a left-handed version. It was the obvious choice.

Now ... the reason for the dynamics above is that producing such an instrument is quite a tightrope to walk from a manufacturing standpoint. We would have loved to have been able to introduce *all* right-handed models as lefties as well, but this just is not typically feasible from a cost perspective. That certainly didn't stop us from always looking for ways to achieve it.

Available in three colors, this guitar did allow left-handed players a way to get in on the action of this new series of instruments. It came in this traditional 3-color sunburst, Chrome Silver and Montego Black. We also offered the 50th Anniversary models left-handed for 2004: both the American Series 50th and the American Deluxe 50th Anniversary seen on previous pages. Additional left-handed guitar and bass models came later in the year.

American Deluxe Series Stratocaster® FMT - From my perspective, this model came as close to a Custom Shop production model guitar as anything we had ever made. This model sat at the top of the new American Deluxe Series of guitars.

Cosmetically this guitar was visually stunning, what with its ebony fingerboard and 2-piece bookmatched flame maple top laminated on an alder body. It was truly a work of art, and another great Fender master-level musical tool.

It was always fun to look at an instrument as it was being packaged up to ship. I got to see a few of these in the factory, fresh off the production line, and remember standing there in awe. It is a fact, that no two-piece bookmatched flame or quilted maple tops are the same. One could say that these were all one-offs, though of course, *every* guitar is unique in its own way.

Customers bought these instruments and displayed them in their homes. Music store owners bought them and displayed them in their music stores.

But the model didn't merely serve as a display piece. It boasted state-of-the-art functionality to match its beauty and elegance. This guitar used the same pickups featured in the Stratocaster HSS, those being the DH-1 humbucking pickup in the bridge position and two SC-NLS ("Samarium Cobalt Noiseless") Strat® pickups in the middle and neck positions. It also included the S-1™ switch housed in the crown of the volume knob just like the other American models that featured S-1™ switching. Although it utilized an LSR Roller Nut and locking tuners like the American Deluxe HSS LT, it did not use the locking bridge found on the HSS LT model. The reason we opted for this approach on this model (as well as the QMT model) was to simply make string changing a slightly easier endeavor.

We released both the FMT (Flame Maple Top) and QMT (Quilted Maple Top) at this time. The models were available in the following colors: Tobacco Sunburst (shown here), Amber, Bing Cherry Transparent and Cobalt Blue Transparent.

American Deluxe Series Stratocaster® QMT - This QMT (Quilted Maple Top) version completed the series on the new American Deluxe Series Stratocaster offering. Part of the challenge of producing nice maple top guitars is to "bookmatch" the two pieces of maple. When done properly, the individual pieces of maple should mirror one another as shown in these photos. If they don't, they cannot be used to create the top. Both the FMT and the QMT were purchased by guitar enthusiasts who wanted a great sounding instrument but were equally enamored with the visual elegance of Fender® art at its finest.

If a Custom Shop instrument was something to aspire to, this was about as close as you were going to get to it in a production model. I got the opportunity to speak to a few folks that bought these guitars at the NAMM Show when we introduced them. When I asked customers why they were interested in this model, a typical response that I got was: "I'm going to hang it in a glass showcase in my office". The QMT model was exactly the same as the FMT in terms of feature, and it was available in the same colors. These colors were Cobalt Blue Transparent (shown here), Amber and Bing Cherry Transparent.

Interestingly enough, Bill Mendello (retired Chairman and CEO of Fender) kept this very guitar and hung it in a glass case in his office. I admittedly derived a bit of pride from the knowledge that the two owners of our company each had guitars that I had done on display in their offices.

American Deluxe Series Stratocaster® "V" Neck - When Dan Smith (Sr. Vice President of R & D) and I sat down to redesign the American Deluxe Series, we started out the old-fashioned way, standing in front of a big white board. We began with a tier structure and worked our way through each proposed model until we had a basic outline of feature sets for each. This particular guitar stemmed from the recordbreaking number of Eric Clapton signature model guitars that we had sold. The famous Fender® "V" neck had always been popular with the Classic '50s crowd of players.

While the original neck shapes were described as a "U" shape on the Telecaster and '51 P-Bass, the original neck shape was called a "C" shape on the new '54 Stratocaster when it premiered. As was the case with any new and unproven model, players who bought them were asked for their feedback. Leo Fender always did this as he was not really a player himself and hence was particular tuned in on player and industry feedback. While the "C" shape endured and eventually became the basis for the standard Fender modern C-shape on many models, the fact is that the neck shape on the Stratocaster varied between '55 and '57. And that is the period when the "V" neck shape first emerged. A fair number of players liked it. In 1957, the "V" neck shape became a standard on the Stratocaster, but that evolved over time as well.

Although this neck shape was favored by many, it wasn't really available on many American made production models with the exception of the '57 American Vintage Reissue — and that guitar has a 7.25" neck radius. We saw an opportunity to give classic Strat® players that old-school neck feel, with the modern day appointments that we had worked to perfect over the years. The primary distinguishing feature on this model from the other new American Deluxe models was the neck shape. It was still a 9.5" radius neck, which had become standard with most Fender models.

In addition, as a means of complementing the "V" neck, we used colors and pickguard materials that echoed the classic '50s vibe and applied a vintage tint finish on the neck itself. This model came with a maple fingerboard, specifically targeted to this market of players. These guitars came in 2-tone Sunburst, Black, Candy Apple Red and Honey Blonde (shown here with a copper-colored pickguard. We always matched body colors with complementary pickguard colors. American made instruments all included hardshell cases at the time, with the exception of Highway 1 instruments which came with a deluxe gig bag.

American Deluxe Series Stratocaster® Ash -
Over the years there have been many studies done to determine as to what kinds of woods sound the best when making guitars. At the end of the day the answer still seems to be subjective. That's because there are too many variables that go into making an instrument. Then of course it comes down to the person playing it. How many times have you witnessed a person playing an instrument that appeared to be of inferior quality make it sound amazing? Too many times for me to count personally.

In the early days of Fender®, ash was readily available. In fact, much of it was derived from the swamps in the south-east. Hence the term "Swap Ash". Later, alder became more readily available (and still is) for the most part. Alder remains very consistent from body spread to body spread while ash isn't necessarily so much that way. Of course, every piece of wood that comes through the Fender factory had to be approved to be worthy of using it to make an instrument.

This extension of the American Deluxe Series gave the player his choice of alder or ash for this instrument as well as all of the new attributes of the American Deluxe Series guitars. This guitar also came with the new S-1™ switching and the new SCN pickups incorporated into it as well. Because ash is a visually more appealing piece of wood, transparent finishes are typically used.

This model was also available with a rosewood or maple fingerboard and we offered it in a left-handed model as well. The colors that this model came in were Aged Cherry Burst (shown here), Butterscotch Blonde and Tobacco Sunburst. It was available in a rosewood or maple neck and or fingerboard.

American Deluxe Series Telecaster® - As Fender® guys, we all knew how particular Tele® players tend to be. After all, a Telecaster has always had a uniquely identifiable and coveted sound. A fair amount of time was invested in the specific pickups made only for this new model. We included two new Samarium Cobalt Noiseless Tele pickups and the S-1™ switching system. These two SC-NLS Tele pickups were listened to, tested and voiced by our in-house Tele players. Of course, they all tended to speak of the merit and tradition of ash bodies on the Telecaster, but we separated that feedback from the testing at hand here.

The S-1 switch made three additional tones available to this Telecaster, which marked a first for traditional Tele players. We also added a chromed stainless-steel bridge, with chrome plated solid brass bridge saddles. When it comes to a Telecaster sound, the bridge and bridge saddles are key in producing that revered tone that only a Telecaster can achieve. Brass bridge saddles have always been synonymous with real-deal Telecaster tone.

These features, in combination with the newly designed pickups, really accentuated the chimey tone that the Telecaster is famous for. The modern C-shape neck was used on this model and the guitar was available with either a rosewood or maple fingerboard. This model shown has an alder body, but as you will see, we did make it available with an ash body as well. Originally it came out in 3-color Sunburst (shown here), Aged Cherry Burst, Montego Black and Candy Tangerine.

As we introduced a variety of new color offerings with this series, we of course developed our own favorites — one of which was always Candy Tangerine. While this finish eventually went away on the American Deluxe Stratocaster, we kept it for a while on this Telecaster. It remains available as an option both in the Custom Shop and Mod Shop. Longtime Fender "web guy" Brad Traweek still frequently cites Candy Tangerine as his favorite Fender color and owns the first Candy Tangerine Mod Shop instrument.

American Deluxe Series Telecaster® Ash - Since we had an ash version of the American Deluxe Stratocaster®, it naturally only made sense to introduce a Tele® version as well.

The new American Deluxe Series Ash Telecaster was the perfect top-of-the-line, American made ash body Tele — designed and built for players looking for an aesthetically beautiful workhorse guitar. If you are a Tele guy, *this* would be your go-to production model.

The guitar featured the S-1 switching system, and two new Samarium Cobalt Noiseless Tele pickups. These two newly designed SC-NLS pickups were bench-tested in R & D (just like all new Fender pickups) before they were approved to go into a new model. We always had so many expert-level, knowledgeable players to rely on. Our in-house Tele players listened over and over to these pickups, until we felt that they were voiced properly to deliver the ultimate Telecaster tone.

We used a modern chromed stainless-steel Tele bridge with chrome plated solid brass bridge saddles, making this guitar extremely versatile and giving the player something beautiful and superior in classic Fender craftsmanship and tone. This Ash Telecaster guitar featured a '52 Tele "U" shaped maple neck and fingerboard with a vintage tint, abalone position dot inlays and 21 medium jumbo frets.

The two colors this model came in were 2-tone Sunburst with M/M/M pickguard and Butterscotch Blonde with Bakelite Black pickguard (shown here).

American Deluxe Series Telecaster® FMT - This guitar was certainly a far cry from a traditional Telecaster although the objective with this model was to make it visually appealing while still maintaining the traditional Tele® tone. Though the Tele is not typically a humbucker-based guitar, there are models still made ('72 Tele® Deluxe, '72 Tele Custom, '72 Tele Thinline) that utilize a humbucker very effectively in accentuating the tone of a Telecaster.

This "top of the line" American Deluxe production model, made in Corona, used the new S-1 switching to help achieve more traditional Telecaster sounds, because with the S-1 switch the player could split the humbuckers into single coils and work with different pickup configurations in addition to the two basic humbuckers. These Fender® "Enforcer" humbuckers were developed specifically for this model, to work in conjunction with the S-1 switch. Just as with the FMT & QMT Stratocaster in this series, the S-1 switch was hidden and housed in the crown of the volume knob. The guitar had a 3-way pickup selector switch.

Though not a standard traditional Telecaster bridge, this Tele bridge was stainless steel and had stainless steel bridge saddles to preserve that Tele snap and tone.

The guitar had an ebony fingerboard and a two-piece bookmatched flame maple top laminated to an alder body. The FMT version came in Bing Cherry Transparent (shown here), Tobacco Sunburst, Amber and Cobalt Blue Transparent.

American Deluxe Series Telecaster® QMT - Custom Shop guitar, you ask? Nope! At the time I showed this production model QMT (Quilted Maple Top) guitar at the NAMM Show, Mike Eldred, our Custom Shop Marketing Manager, brought over his team of Custom Shop builders and had them take a look at this instrument. For me, there was naturally a definite sense of pride. To have those guys whom I all admired so much, compliment me on this model was hugely appreciated.

Of course, I didn't *build* it; my job was to oversee creating it and bringing it to market. It was a stunning example of Fender® production line capabilities. Doesn't the picture here say it all? I heard countless compliments from customers and the general public throughout the four-day run of the show.

As stated previously with the FMT model, the QMT model also used the "Enforcer" humbuckers developed specifically for these models, with the S-1 switching giving the player a wide variety of Tele tone choices.

When it comes to the Telecaster and the people that play the Tele, they tend to be very strategic about their tone. A bold statement there, because *all* players are, of course ... but Tele players are uniquely so. And, this guitar fit the bill and fit very nicely into an existing Tele player's arsenal.

The specifications of this model mirrored those of the FMT model. Like the FMT version, the QMT version came in Amber (shown here), Bing Cherry Transparent, Tobacco Sunburst and Cobalt Blue Transparent.

Classic Series '72 Telecaster® Deluxe - This was an exciting guitar to reissue. One method we used to decide on older models to reissue was to sift through old Fender® catalogs. After I would look at a model in an old catalog, I would look for it on eBay. The potential demand for the product would be readily apparent. Or not, as the case might be. When I looked at the going prices for these Tele Deluxe guitars it was obvious to me that people wanted them.

When I approached Dan Smith (SR. VP of Fender R & D) about doing this model, he laughed a bit at me. His comment to me was something along the lines of: "those guitars failed miserably back in the '70s, so why would we make that mistake again"? I pushed forward in this case. After all, it was my decision and the results would be mine to bear as well. My hunch proved accurate and it quickly became one of Fender's more popular selling Telecaster models.

The model is unique for a couple of reasons. First it actually has a Stratocaster® headstock. One of the things Fender's legal counsel was in the process of pursuing at this time was pursuing a trademark on the traditional Stratocaster headstock shape of the '50s and 60s. Mark Van Vleet (our chief counsel) accomplished that; however because of this, the release of this guitar required careful consideration.

The neck has a flat 12-inch radius. and the humbucking pickups were originally designed by Seth Lover. At the time back in 1972, the idea behind this guitar was to compete with that certain other name brand company who owned the market with humbucker equipped guitars. The pickups were marketed at that time as "Wide Range Humbuckers", so when we decided to reissue this guitar, these pickups were replicated by our Fender R & D team.

Back in '72, executives from CBS had been trying to implement new "models" by leveraging knowledge of veteran Fender employees who knew more about what could or could not be made at that time. They tended to use the parts that they had on hand at the time. They had plenty of Stratocaster necks available, and so it only made sense to give it a shot.

The reissue of this model survived for three years before it was discontinued, but after 30 years of obscurity it was brought back to life and resurfaced as a popular and unique-sounding Fender. So ... perhaps a lesson learned?

This model came in Black, 3-color Sunburst, Walnut Stain and included a Fender deluxe gig bag.

Deluxe Series Aerodyne™ Stratocaster® -
The Aerodyne Bass had been released in January of the previous year and had met with great success. I had been looking at the Aerodyne Strat® and Tele® from this series for a while. It was time to bring these two instruments into the states.

We released this Stratocaster as well as the Telecaster® to complete the Aerodyne series. One of the things that made these guitars (and the bass) unique was the top. It had a radius-carved top, the first of its kind on a Fender® guitar. This had simply never been done on a Fender Stratocaster or Telecaster before. It featured cream binding on top of a basswood body (also unique) and a matching black headstock. Our factories in Corona and Mexico did not typically use Basswood for guitar bodies but not because of the common misnomer that it doesn't sound good. It *does*, and though all sound is subjective, in my opinion as well as many other people's, it actually sounds reminiscent of mahogany.

The maple neck had a rosewood fingerboard with 22 medium jumbo frets. The fingerboard radius of the neck was the older, traditional 7.25" but because of the larger frets, string bending was an easy function for players. It had chrome hardware and used the standard vintage-style bridge commonly used on specific Fender Japan models. This guitar used three ST-Vintage Fender single coils with individually adjusted pole pieces, designed by Fender Japan R & D engineers. They were great sounding classic vintage Fender single-coil pickups. The silver appliqué logo along with the chrome hardware really added the finishing touches to this sleek looking instrument.

Aerodyne Stratocaster Radius-Carved Top

Deluxe Series Aerodyne™ Telecaster® - The Aerodyne Telecaster completed the new family of Aerodyne ("aerodynamic") instruments.

While we had been making P-90-style pickups at that time and implementing them into models such as the Strat-o-sonic, that pickup and its name was evolving and it was called the Black Dove and Black Dove II, but these actually had nothing to do with this particular model.

Instead, the Japanese factory where these models came from had great R & D people of their own who designed great pickups based on traditional Fender pickup specifications.

The specifications were of course very similar to the Stratocaster® except for the obvious Tele-specific differences. This guitar utilized one TL-Vintage (Bridge) pickup and one HOTROD-T (Neck) pickup; the P-90 style neck pickup really opened up additional tonal possibilities for the Tele® player.

Our use of a steel Tele bridge with 6 individually adjustable bridge saddles allowed for perfect intonation. Overall: a nice looking, great-sounding and ergonomically comfortable guitar to play. It quickly became another go-to model for Tele players.

Both of these instruments were light weight and very resonant. Not surprising as these are typical characteristics of basswood.

Aerodyne Telecaster Radius Carved Top

Special Edition Series Lite Ash Stratocaster® - In early 2004, Bill Schultz called me to his office and told me he wanted me to get to the Cort® factory in Korea and work on designing some new Fender® guitars.

Previously we met with great success with a few models that this factory was making for us: namely the Custom Telecaster® HH FMT that we had done in January of 2003. I had been working with the folks at Cort for quite some time, as many of the Squier models were manufactured at their Indonesian factory. The quality of the products that they were producing in their Korean factory was more than up to the standards required to put the Fender name on. I had put together several models in my head and down on paper and was speaking weekly with the folks at Cort about what I wanted to see. I planned my trip and flew over to spend a week to work on these projects. When I arrived at the factory, all of the guitars I had been talking to these folks about were already on display in the conference room.

However, this guitar was NOT one of them. I hadn't even considered this particular guitar up to this point. It was important in my mind to make sure that the initial models coming out of Korea would be differentiated from Fender North American guitars. That's why we started out with things like the Special Edition Esquire, and the Showmaster® Celtic and Scorpion models and continued to expand the Showmaster offering. However, when I walked through the factory, I picked up an ash body spread and discovered it weighed almost nothing. I then found Birdseye maple neck blanks and the light bulb for this model turned on in my head. This type of exercise in visiting factories are exactly how ideas for models are born.

The American made Seymour Duncan pickups that we used on this Stratocaster model were an APS-1™ narrow spacing Alnico II Pro staggered (neck), an APS-1™RWRP (reverse wound) narrow spacing Alnico II Pro staggered (middle) and an APS-1™ Alnico II Pro staggered in the (bridge) position. We were now officially and strategically placing American made Seymour Duncan pickups in these new Fender models manufactured by our Korean family partners, as you will see in the following pages. Seymour Duncan created these narrow-spaced middle and neck Strat® pickups specifically for this instrument.

The birdseye maple neck was highly figured with medium jumbo frets, a modern C-shape and 9.5" neck radius (our standard Fender spec). The Lite Ash body, as it was marketed, was literally a 5-pound body by itself and made for a very lightweight instrument when fully assembled. The guitar had chrome hardware and a 2-point pivot tremolo/bridge (like our standard spec American Series Stratocaster). It had a single-ply black pickguard with matching pickup covers, control knobs and switch tip.

Upon its release, the Stratocaster and the Telecaster® came only in Natural Ash (shown), but later Black and Vintage White were added as well.

Special Edition Series Lite Ash Telecaster® -

This model was another example of a Korean made Fender® model that incorporated American-made Seymour Duncan® pickups. Fender had (and still has) a long-standing relationship with the Seymour Duncan company. Seymour was always a Tele player and designed the famous Tele-Gib guitar Jeff Beck used on *Blow by Blow*.

For these guitars, I really started working closely with Seymour Duncan's Evan Skopp. Evan was an executive in the company and played in Seymour's band. He was often referred to as Seymour's "right hand." Evan was key in choosing the Seymour Duncan pickups that went into these instruments.

We had been using Seymour Duncan pickups in Fender guitars for a long time. We had used "Duncan Designed" pickups on Squier® models — but with the Fender branded guitars, we used the more expensive American made Seymour Duncan pickups to round out the feature set on these guitars.

The Tele® used an APTR-1 Alnico II Pro (neck) position pickup and an APTL-1 Alnico II Pro (bridge) position pickup. These American made Seymour Duncan pickups were voiced by Evan specifically for this guitar as well as these others. Being a Tele guy as Evan was, after we finished with this project, Evan actually bought this very guitar.

The other challenge that I had in Korea while looking for the right components for these two models, was finding brass barrel bridge saddles for this Telecaster. While visiting another Cort manufacturing facility, we discovered that they were indeed available, so we implemented them onto this Telecaster bridge. The guitar was now ready for production.
The model was available in Natural Ash (as shown), with Black and Vintage White added as additional options later.

The factory was under strict orders to ensure that all bodies remained under an agreed-upon light weight (even as a fully assembled instrument), thus the "Lite Ash" name for these Special Edition models.

Special Edition Series TC-90 Thinline Telecaster® - This guitar was a project that Dan Smith (Sr. VP of R & D) had in his back pocket for a while. Through his years at Fender®, Dan had designed many guitars for the company. Dan was also a big Telecaster fan and this guitar was one that he had on the drawing board. When I asked him to show it to me, we discussed what options that we had to bring this guitar to market. There would be several challenges that we would be faced with that just wouldn't allow us to justify the ROI. The immediate solution that we came up with was to have Cort Korea make it for us. Dan had the CAD drawings for it, so it would be easy for them to plug the drawings into their CNC machines and build us a sample. This is precisely what they did and after a few minor tweaks, we were ready to have it scheduled for production.

This guitar consisted of a chambered ash body, with 22 medium jumbo frets, and a 24 ¾" scale length set neck. We used two American Seymour Duncan® P-90 pickups.

The SP90-1 neck position pickup had that distinctive gutsy P-90 sound, faithfully duplicating every detail in sound, construction and appearance.

The SP90-3 bridge position pickup had specially designed ceramic magnets and a custom coil configuration, giving an outstanding full frequency response and maximum output. The neck and bridge pickups were specially calibrated for their positions, to compensate for the different string vibration in the two positions.

The guitar came with a vintage-style Adjust-o-matic bridge with anchored tailpiece, smoked chrome hardware, and abalone dot inlays. It had a modern C-shape 9.5" radius maple neck with a rosewood fingerboard, and a 3-ply B/W/B pickguard.

It came in Black Cherry Burst (shown here) and Vintage White. Later this model was replaced by the signature model Jim Adkins JA-90 Telecaster which of course was slightly different — but Jim cited his love of this TC-90 as the inspiration for creating his own version of the guitar, which remains in the Fender lineup today.

Special Edition Series Telecaster® Blackout - In continuing to develop our new series of Fender® imported instruments and looking to fill holes and requests from consumers, we included the release of this model. My target customer for this guitar was the younger rock player. In the world of electric guitars, black has been and will always be the most popular color. The various instruments that we were developing in Korea were primarily all set neck guitars with the exception of the Lite Ash Stratocaster® and Telecaster. The Telecaster and Showmaster shown here were both set necks.

We used side position dot markers on this model and as you can see, everything else was black. Since the Cort factory had nice lightweight basswood available, we decided to use it on this model. The body was a flat top slab body, made of basswood, which was light weight and very resonant.

Included was a Seymour Duncan® SH-1N RP '59 reverse polarity neck position humbucker (neck position), and a Seymour Duncan SHPGP-1B Pearly Gates Plus humbucker in the bridge position. The bridge was a 6-saddle string-through-body hardtail design, placing an emphasis on sustain and resonance.

Our Fender neck standards for most of our electric guitars were/are a modern C-shape profile and 9.5-inch radius fingerboard with medium jumbo frets. This series of Special Editions all used these specs and had 22 frets with the exception of the Lite Ash Strat® and Tele® which were 21-fret necks. The controls were a volume, tone and a 3-way selector switch.

With the introduction of these models, we began using oversized strap buttons. The idea was to eliminate the need for strap locks. Once you got your favorite strap on, it was not easy to get it to come off.

The "Blackout" guitars were part of the Special Edition Series and came in Black and Atlantic Blue Metallic.

Special Edition Series Showmaster® FAT SSS - While visiting Korean factories I looked at different types of woods that were readily available at that time. Wood options come and go over time and keeping conscious of environmental impact and global resources has always been something important to Fender®.

I had never seen flamed ash before and thought that this looked great. I listened to the wood as used on samples in the Korean factory and liked how it sounded, so we used it on these two new Showmaster models. We called it "FAT", which stood for Flame Ash Top. The top was laminated to a basswood body. The use of basswood for the body was important to keep the overall weight of the guitar reasonable. On all of our new imported Showmaster guitars we used a modern C-shape maple set neck with a 15.75" radius, making for a notably flatter rosewood fingerboard. The Showmaster guitars all featured 24 jumbo frets and abalone dot inlays as well.

The pickups were American made Seymour Duncan® pickups consisting of an SSL52-1 5-2 (neck) position, an SSL52-1 5-2 RWRP (middle) position and an SSL52-1B 5-2 (bridge) position, plus five-position switching. These pickups used a novel approach that combined alnico 5 magnets on the bass strings and alnico 2 magnets on the treble strings. The idea was originally conceived of by Nashville repairman to the stars, Joe Glaser, who had built similar (Tele) pickups for Brent Mason. The Seymour Duncan company originally released these pickups as the Nashville Session series, but then realized that that name pigeonholed the pickups. The name was eventually changed to Five-Two to widen the market appeal, and yet effectively capture the fact that the pickups used two different types of magnets.

Other features included smoked-chrome hardware, knurled knobs, a graphite nut and a two-point pivot tremolo/bridge. This guitar came in the Cherry Sunburst finish shown here.

Special Edition Series Showmaster® FAT HH - While the Fender® Showmaster prior to this point had only been made in our Custom Shop, it was a non-traditional Fender platform. The guitars were incredibly well built like all of our Custom Shop instruments were, but they were also expensive and obviously quite different from the traditional Fender iconic platform models the Custom Shop was so famous for. I had had success in my prior position as the Squier Marketing Manager using the Showmaster name so using it now on these new models with our Fender logo felt right.

The aim was to have the guitars created overseas and distributed as less expensive Fender models. Shown here is the same version of the FAT (flame ash top) Showmaster in the two-humbucker version.

The Seymour Duncan® pickups used on this guitar were two of the most popular pickups they had designed for Fender: an SHPGP-1B Pearly Gates Plus humbucker (bridge position) and an SH-1N RP '59 reverse polarity humbucker (neck position).

The six models in the Special Edition Series used basswood for the bodies. The specifications were a three-way switch to select either pickup, or both at the same time. Aside from the pickups, the specs were identical to the SSS version. Same features, using a modern C-shape maple set neck with a 15.75" radius and rosewood fingerboard, 24 jumbo frets and abalone dot inlays. Smoked-chrome hardware, knurled knobs, a graphite nut and a 2-point pivot tremolo/bridge. Cherry Sunburst was the finish.

Special Edition Series Showmaster® QBT SSS - Another wood I looked at and decided to use was quilted bubinga. Bubinga has been used for years to build guitars, particularly by acoustic guitar builders. Bubinga, because of its woodgrain composition, has tonal characteristics similar to mahogany but also has a unique visual aesthetic appeal. Aside from the top material and the color, this instrument had the same specifications as its brother, the FAT SSS.

I worked closely with Evan Skopp at Seymour Duncan® in developing all of the Seymour Duncan pickups for use on our Fender® guitars made in Korea at that time. Like its counterpart, the FAT SSS, this guitar used an SSL52-1 5-2 (neck position), an SSL52-1 5-2 RWRP (middle position) and an SSL52-1B 5-2 (bridge position), plus five-position switching. Same features, using a modern C-shape maple set neck with a 15.75" radius, rosewood fingerboard, 24 jumbo frets and abalone dot inlays. Other features include smoked-chrome hardware, knurled knobs, a graphite nut and a 2-point pivot tremolo/bridge.

When considering colors to use, experimentation is important. After all, if an instrument isn't visually appealing, its marketability substantially reduces accordingly. The Brown Transparent finish on this model really allowed the Bubinga to "pop" from a visual standpoint. I had seen it on drum sets before and it had looked good on them, so we tried it on this model and it worked out really well.

Special Edition Series Showmaster® QBT HH - I remember working on this particular guitar at the factory in Korea. Being right there in the factory itself, we were surrounded by factory engineers and their R & D group. As their largest account, we had 100% of their attention. They always treated us very well and our working relationship was a strong one.

On this particular guitar, we were getting it dialed in but I was not happy with the neck heel, feeling that it had too much of a hump; and since this was a set neck guitar, I wanted the access to the higher registers to be smooth and effortless. Since we had translators with us, I could easily convey to the factory what I was trying to accomplish. In this case when I expressed my point, the factory engineers grabbed the guitar and reappeared a half hour later with the neck heel sanded down and contoured exactly the way that I wanted it. Once this spec shape was decided upon, it became the new spec for all of the new Showmaster models. Of course, this was prior to any of these guitars being released, so this "new" spec change was only new to *us* and just part of the process of finalizing and signing off on these models before going into production.

The naming convention began to take shape as the models evolved, these becoming the "QBT", using quilted bubinga for the top wood as well as the SSS version.

The Seymour Duncan® pickups used on this guitar were an SHPGP-1B Pearly Gates Plus humbucker (bridge position) and an SH-1N RP '59 reverse polarity humbucker (neck position).

The guitar featured a 3-way switch to select either pickup, or both at the same time. Aside from the pickups, the specs were identical to the SSS version. Same features, using a modern C-shape maple set neck with a 15.75" radius, a rosewood fingerboard, 24 jumbo frets and abalone dot inlays. Smoked-chrome hardware, knurled knobs, a graphite nut and a 2-point pivot tremolo/bridge. Finished in Brown Transparent as shown here.

Special Edition Series Showmaster® Blackout - This model was part of the new Special Edition Showmaster offering and was the brother to the previously seen Telecaster® Blackout. Everything on this model was black, and we used side position dot markers as opposed to dot markers on the fretboard, targeting younger rock-'n'-roll customers.

You may notice that this early picture does not show the Seymour Duncan® logo on the pickups. This is simply because the photo is of one of the early prototypes, before we finalized production, implementing the SHPGP-1B Pearly Gates Plus humbucker (bridge} and the the SH-1N RP 59 reverse polarity humbucker (neck) that came on this model when it was released.

The guitar also utilized a 3-way switch to select either pickup, or both at the same time. Same features as the other Showmaster models, using a modern C-shape maple set neck with a 15.75" radius, which is a notably-flatter, a rosewood fingerboard, 24 jumbo frets and abalone dot inlays. The black hardware, knurled knobs, graphite nut and a 2-point pivot tremolo/bridge, completed the specs for these two new Fender "Blackout" models.

This model came in Black and Atlantic Blue Metallic, just like its Telecaster Blackout brother.

Standard Series Stratocaster® HH - At this point in time we did not have a dual humbucker Stratocaster in our Standard Series. We knew that we sold a large number of guitars with a humbucking pickup in the bridge position between the Standard Strat HSS and Standard Strat HSS w/original Floyd Rose® tremolo. It was time for us to offer a two-humbucker version of the Standard Stratocaster.

It was always very easy to "overthink" any model we were considering, particularly considering one could build just about anything one could dream up, making the possibilities near endless. However, this particular model seemed like a bit of a "no brainer", to to speak, as our research told us this Standard Series Stratocaster HH was sure to be embraced.

The specifications were very similar to the standard Stratocaster with the obvious exception of the pickups themselves. The guitar featured two Tex-Mex Fat Strat humbucking pickups. Constructed with alnico 5 magnets and polysol magnet wire with 4-conductor wiring, this Tex-Mex humbucker provided increased string response with a warm, full-bodied output. Although this pickup was already available as an aftermarket accessory from Fender and Fender dealers, it was only available in white, so we made it in black specifically for this new model. We also thought we would make this model look a little bit different and went with a 3-ply B/W/B pickguard, black knobs, switch tip and a tremolo arm tip. The guitar utilized a 3-way switch to select either pickup, or both at the same time. It had the same features as most of our Fender guitars, with a modern C-shape maple neck and 9.5" radius (our standard Fender spec). This model specifically came with a rosewood fingerboard only, our research indicating that generally speaking, humbucker seeking players leaned more towards rosewood fingerboards.

The guitar came in the same colors as the Standard Stratocaster at that time, however in further differentiating this model from the Standard Strat model, we chose to use a poly satin finish on this model as opposed to a gloss finish. The colors were the same as the Standard Stratocaster which were Black, Sage Green Metallic, Blue Agave, Brown Sunburst, Arctic White and Midnight Wine (shown here). The guitar sold for the same price as the Standard Stratocaster.

Artist Series Roscoe Beck Bass IV - Being the captain of the ship for Fender® Electric guitars is one thing but the gig also included taking ownership of the basses as well. This was no easy task because I was not and am not a bass player (though I do love playing bass). It was a great education to learn and speak the language of bass players.

Most players knew Roscoe because of his history playing with Eric Johnson, however his body of work also included playing and recording with other artists such as Robben Ford, Leonard Cohen, and the Vaughan brothers, as well as other top artists.

The 5-string version was initially introduced into the Fender Artist Series bass lineup in 1995. This 4-string version, pictured here, was now added to the lineup.

Roscoe Beck already had his signature series bass, but he contacted me to discuss some upgrades and changes that he wanted to make to his existing bass. He flew out to the office to meet with us. Whenever I worked on a bass project, I involved several of our top-notch employees and bass players at the office. We had several guys that were experts at the office. One in particular was a gentleman named Bob Willocks. Bob and I had become good friends over the years and he was involved in many projects at Fender but more than anything, he was a bass-playing professional that had great insight into Fender basses. Working with Roscoe, Bob and Dan Smith, we implemented these changes to this bass and released it in January of 2004.

Some of the upgrades to Roscoe's existing bass were: an expanded cutaway on the G-string side for easier access to upper registers, a graphite reinforced maple neck with rosewood fingerboard, and Bill Lawrence designed pickups. We used dome-style "Tele®" knobs and a new parchment pickguard, and his signature was moved from the headstock to the neckplate. Included were Ultralite Hipshot® tuning machines, with a de-tuner on the E-string tuning gear, as well as a Hipshot® triple string tree and a newly designed bridge.

The Roscoe Beck models were eventually discontinued in 2009.

Artist Series Mike Dirnt Precision Bass® - The original Mike Dirnt P Bass® was built by Alex Perez, Custom Shop builder and artist relations guru. Mike Dirnt? Yes, THE Mike Dirnt of Green Day. Alex called me to tell me that in speaking with Mike, he wanted to create his own signature model bass in our factory and offer it to everyone. Mike and Alex flew to Scottsdale and we had lunch together as we began to discuss how we were going to make this happen. Although Billie Joe Armstrong, the voice and guitarist for this 3-piece powerhouse, was the face of Green Day, many people did not realize that Mike Dirnt was the driving force behind the band.

At that time, Green Day was back together after having just taken a few years off. Mike was excited about this bass, but he was also quite excited about the recent reunion of his band. I remember him telling us how the magic was back and the band had just recorded about 20 new pre-production songs. I could see the fire in his eyes. Those songs later became the tunes on *American Idiot*, the band's biggest-selling album of all time. Of course, at that time no one knew that Green Day was about to explode into the upper stratosphere of commercial success and that *American Idiot* would even become a Broadway musical.

After lunch with Mike and Alex, we headed back to the office and I introduced Mike to a group of people who would help execute his vision. When asked about the "star" tattooed on his arm he told us it stood for his daughter, Stella. He wanted that star on the neckplate of his new bass. Designer Clay Lyons grabbed a camera and took a photo of Mike's tattoo on his arm. Clay then replicated Mike's tattoo in Photoshop so that manufacturing could make a neckplate with Stella's name on it. The "Star" was born.

Mike is a very astute business/marketing professional. A few months later when we launched Mike's new model at the January NAMM show, Mike was there. There were crowds of people around him at that show. Fender dealers took this model seriously and placed orders for it enthusiastically.

Mike's model was discussed, planned (based on the original Custom Shop specs), and would be manufactured in our Mexico factory, making it extremely affordable. This bass was somewhat similar to a '51 P Bass, but Mike wanted a Bad Ass II bridge on it. It has an ash slab body (like a '51) with a '55 P Bass arm contour. We used Custom Shop '59 P Bass pickups. Of course, a '51 P Bass was an all maple neck with a Modern-C-Shape neck profile, but Mike wanted a rosewood fretboard. At the time we released this bass it was available in 2-tone sunburst, Black and Vintage White (shown here). It has evolved through the years but is still a part of the Fender family of instruments.

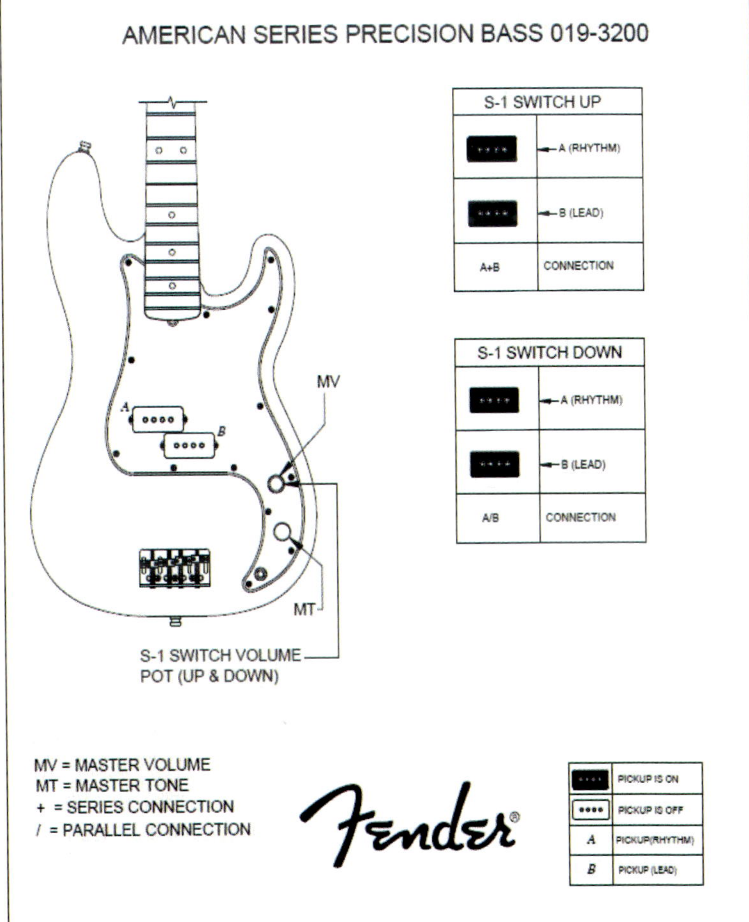

American Deluxe Series P Bass® & Jazz Bass® W/ S-1™ Switch - With the new S-1™ switch, the P Bass® & Jazz Bass® opened up some cool tonal variances on the traditional sound usually achieved with these two iconic bass platforms.

The picture at left shows the S-1 switch housed in the crown of the volume knob of the American Deluxe Jazz Bass.

While the P Bass® has pickups that always run in series, pressing the S-1™ switch put them in parallel giving the P Bass a snappier, almost Jazz Bass type of tone. The same holds true for the Jazz Bass, but the pickups are designed to run in parallel.

And as for the Jazz Bass, When the S-1™ switch is pressed it combined the pickups in series giving the Jazz Bass a thicker, almost P Bass kind of tone.

Since the S-1™ switch was new, our goal at that time was to incorporate it into our new American Deluxe Series and our newer American made instruments where it made the most sense. In this case the switch was used not only on the new American Deluxe Series guitars, but also on the American Series of basses.

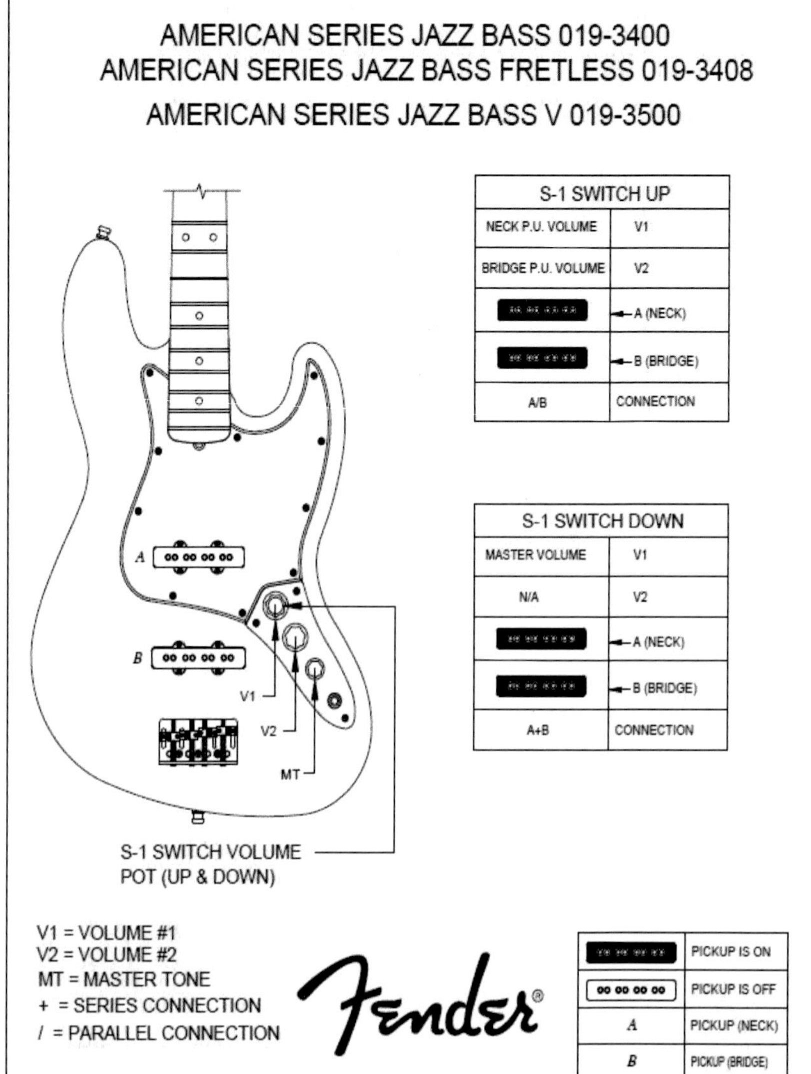

And as for the Jazz Bass, When the S-1™ switch is pressed it combined the pickups in series giving the Jazz Bass a thicker, almost P Bass kind of tone.

Having new total flexibility on classic iconic basses because of the new S-1™ switching was a first and simply gave Fender bass players more.

We incorporate it into our new American Deluxe Series guitars, our new American Deluxe Series basses, as well as newer American Series guitars and basses where it made the most sense. In this case the switch shows the new American Deluxe Series Jazz Bass® and its new functionality.

American Deluxe Series Precision Bass® - There are so many bass playing legends that laid down the foundation for iconic songs using the Precision Bass. James Jamerson was a great example of one of those players, delivering perfectly-crafted bass lines from his '61 Precision Bass and using them to drive songs that became #1 hit records.

The relaunch of the American Deluxe Series naturally meant innovation for both guitars and basses. If a Precision Bass back in the '50s could have been built in a "Custom Shop," so to speak, then this top-of-the-line Precision Bass would have been it. This is the first of the basses as we began implementing the newly designed samarium cobalt pickups, which incorporated the new S-1 switching as shown on the previous pages.

The upgrades started with the Samarium Cobalt Noiseless pickups. Our R & D spent a number of hours voicing these pickups specifically for bass, just as we had done with guitars. The pickups consisted of one Split SC-P (middle) & one HB-1 (bridge). These pickups were as quiet as anything we had ever done before.

The other upgrades included a new 18-volt active, 3-band EQ, a newly designed top-load or string-through-body bridge with a chromed steel bridge plate and nickel-plated brass saddles for better tone and sustain.

Additional upgrades were a 5-bolt neckplate with a contoured heel, allowing even better access to the higher register frets, and a graphite reinforced neck. We also implemented new lightweight tuners with a lower gear ratio for precise tuning and a smooth feel. These were definitive upgrades to the new American Deluxe Series of basses.

This photo is of the alder body, although we offered it in ash as well as we'll see in upcoming pages. It featured a modern C-Shape neck profile and was available with either a rosewood or maple fingerboard. The standard modern C-Shape neck profile was incorporated, and nut width of the 4-string bass was 1.625".

The S-1 switching diagrams seen on the previous pages show how this new technology functioned and applied to all of this new crop of American Deluxe Series basses.
Lastly, in keeping with the idea of offering a visual variety of choices for the player, we produced these basses in different colors and pickguard combinations such as Amber, w/Brown Shell, Montego Black w/Gold Vinyl, Chrome Silver, w/Silver Shell, as well the traditional color of 3-tone Sunburst w/W/B/W 3-ply pickguard as seen here.

American Deluxe Series Precision Bass® V - The New American Deluxe P Bass® V was identical to the P Bass® IV in specs, features and upgrades except we used Pao Ferro as an option instead of Rosewood for the fingerboard. Although this 5-string model was available with a Pao Ferro fingerboard, a maple fingerboard was available as well. We also used two Hipshot® string trees with custom tailored break-angles to create a balanced string tension across all five strings. These were the only differences between the 4 and 5 string Precision basses.

The bass as we have always known it, most frequently refers to a 4-string configuration, although there are not many bass players who haven't picked up and played a 5-string or even 6-string bass. World re-nowned bass players have used a 5-string bass at some point in their career, whether when recording a song, or using it live, or in some cases making it their standard go-to instrument. It's that low "B" string that brings the extra-low frequency and basically gives the bassist five extra low notes that can be used. The 5-string bass is a go-to for Marcus Miller, for example; the 5-string configuration is simply what he plays regularly, period. (His signature model was seen on a previous page.)

The nut width on a 5-string bass is slightly wider than that of the 4-string equivalent. The actual nut width on Fender 5-string basses is 1.875".

Although "tone" is always subjective to one's individual ears, just as with guitars when it comes to bass body wood characteristics, alder tends to have a pronounced midrange and was used on 80% of Fender bass bodies.

This 5-String model was available in 3-color Sunburst with M/B/M pickguard, Amber with Brown Shell pickguard and Montego Black with a Gold Vinyl pickguard - and as was with all American made instruments, included a standard hardshell case.

American Deluxe Series Precision Bass® Ash - The specs of the ash body model were of course largely the same as the alder body model. Ash can often make for a heavier body wood, but it offers a strong low end, brighter highs, and not quite as much midrange. These traits make it an advantageous choice both for those looking to "thump" away but also those employing slapping and popping techniques in their playing. As always, tone is subjective! And at Fender®, if the body wood was deemed too heavy, we simply didn't purchase it or use it.

This is the ash version of what was the new American Deluxe P Bass. Ash bodies lent themselves to being suitable for transparent (or semi-transparent) finishes to be able to show off the attractive wood grain. Since most of the early Fender body woods were ash, most of the traditional colors were used, like Butterscotch Blonde seen here.

The bass had a standard modern C-Shape neck profile and nut width typical for a 4-string P Bass (namely, 1.625").

The new Samarium Cobalt Noiseless pickups were the same as those on the alder version of the bass, consisting of one Split SC-P (middle) & one HB-1 (bridge). These P Bass pickups were designed to run in parallel. When the S-1™ switch is pressed it combined the pickups in series giving the P Bass almost Jazz Bass-like tone.

The available colors for the American Deluxe Precision Bass Ash were Aged Cherry Sunburst with W/B/W pickguard, Butterscotch Blonde (shown here) with B/W/B pickguard and Tobacco Sunburst with M/B/M pickguard.

American Deluxe Series Precision Bass® Ash V - This model echoed the same specs as the American Deluxe Precision Bass V, but with an Ash body. Pao Ferro, not Rosewood, was used for the fingerboard, but maple was also an available option. 5-String basses benefit from additional neck support because of the added string tension. It can be achieved by adding an additional truss rod, or in this case adding two Hipshot® string trees with custom tailored break-angles to create a balanced string tension across all five strings.

The new Samarium Cobalt Noiseless pickups were the same as those in the alder version seen earlier, consisting of one Split SC-P 5-string (middle) and a 5-string HB-1 (bridge).

S-1 switching was used on all of these new models, the 5-string basses being no exception. Details on how the S-1 switching functioned on basses is described on previous pages.

The bass had a standard modern C-Shape neck profile and a nut width of 1.875".

The same colors that were available on the ash 4-string were used on the ash 5-string model. They were Aged Cherry Sunburst with W/B/W pickguard, Butterscotch Blonde with B/W/B pickguard and Tobacco Sunburst with M/B/M pickguard.

This picture shows the ash model with a 3-ply shell pickguard (as this was the first sample); however, the final version used a 3-ply W/B/W pickguard.

American Deluxe Series Jazz Bass® - It's no secret that when Fender® launched the Jazz Bass in 1960, it (like its older brother, the Precision Bass) would quickly become a go-to bass for legendary players then and in the future.

Artists like Geddy Lee, Jaco Pastorious and many others declared the Jazz Bass their tool of choice and propelled the instrument to the same level of visibility as had been achieved for the Precision Bass.

The new American Deluxe Jazz Bass featured upgrades that were visually subtle, but effective. The standard nut width of 1.5" for the Jazz Bass did not and has not changed (except on specific models), but the upgrades to this model "under the hood" were significant, opening up a large array of additional tonal choices.

The Jazz Bass looks the same as it did when it hit the market back in March of 1960. True Fender upgrades to this model were not made or even considered early on, but just as with the guitars, Fender did pursue new colors right away as the world was starting to see a new palette of colors emerge on new car production models. This is when we began seeing the following colors become a part of Fender's own color array: Lake Placid Blue, Daphne Blue, Sonic Blue, Shoreline Gold, Olympic White, Burgundy Mist, Black, Sherwood Green, Foam Green, Surf Green, Inca Silver, Fiesta Red, Dakota Red and Shell Pink.

The challenge is that it just isn't reasonable to offer any single model in too many colors at once, so when it came to a model like this there was typically a nod to both traditional finishes while also incorporating newer, unconventional selections. For example: 3-Color Sunburst was offered (as pictured here), and in fact this was the color used on the first Fender Jazz Bass back in 1960. And yet, the offering also included more nonconventional color choices as well: Amber, Montego Black, and Chrome Silver.

The goal with this bass (and all of the new American Deluxe Series instruments) was to give players a choice of colors and pickguards. The idea was to make something visually appealing to all players and offer a top-of-the-line Fender production model Jazz Bass.

These Jazz Bass and Precision Bass models were already well solidified. Our job was to figure meaningful ways to upgrade the features on these icons. The specific upgrades on the new Jazz Bass included an active three-band EQ, and two dual-coil ceramic noiseless Jazz Bass pickups with nickel-plated pole pieces, and the new S-1 switching as shown previously.

This bass was available with either a rosewood or maple fingerboard and came in 3-color Sunburst with M/B/M pickguard (shown here), Amber with Brown Shell pickguard, Montego Black with Gold Vinyl pickguard and Chrome Silver with Silver Shell pickguard. This bass came in a hardshell case.

American Deluxe Series Jazz Bass® V - The 5-string version of the Jazz Bass® was the same as the 4-String Jazz Bass and used a Pao Ferro fingerboard, not rosewood — and a maple fingerboard was available as an option as well. This is the alder body version, but this bass was also available in ash. The Hipshot® string trees with custom tailored break-angles created a balanced string tension across all five strings and were used on all of our 5-string basses in the American Deluxe Series.

The new Samarium Cobalt Noiseless pickups were the same as those on the alder version seen earlier, featuring two SC-NLS 5-string pickups voiced specifically for the 5-string Jazz Bass models.

S-1 switching was used on this model (as with all the new American Deluxe models); details on how the S-1 switching works on these basses is described on a previous page.

The bass had a standard modern C-Shape neck profile and nut width of 1.875".

The available color options were 3-color Sunburst with M/B/M pickguard, Amber with Brown Shell pickguard (shown here), Montego Black with Gold Vinyl pickguard and Candy Tangerine with 4-ply shell pickguard. American Deluxe instruments all included Fender hardshell cases.

American Deluxe Series Jazz Bass® Ash - The new American Deluxe Jazz Bass featured upgrades that were visually subtle but effective. The standard nut width of 1.5" for the Jazz Bass did not and has not changed (except on specific models) and the standard modern C-Shape neck profile remains, but the upgrades to this model "under the hood" were significant, opening up a large array of additional tonal choices. The features of the ash 4-string bass were the same as those of the alder version.

As mentioned previously, the upgrades included an active three-band EQ and two new SC-NLS J dual-coil ceramic noiseless Jazz Bass pickups with nickel-plated pole pieces. The S-1 switching, as shown previously, was also included as part of these upgrades.

The Jazz Bass has not changed much from its original design when it hit the market back in March of 1960. However, ash bodies were truthfully not in active use on the new Jazz Bass or Precision Bass by 1960 — alder was the body wood of choice at that point.

True Fender® upgrades to this model were not made or even considered, because these two icons clearly established the foundation of electric bass.

This bass was available with either a rosewood or maple fingerboard and was available in Aged Cherry Sunburst with W/B/W pickguard (shown here), Butterscotch Blonde with B/W/B pickguard and Tobacco Sunburst with M/B/M pickguard, always selecting pickguard colors to complement the body finishes.

American Deluxe Series Jazz Bass® FMT - The new American Deluxe Jazz Bass FMT/QMT is a stunning piece of classic Fender® craftsmanship made on the production line in Corona. It was as close as we could get to a Custom Shop bass.

Whether you chose the FMT (Flame Maple) or the QMT (Quilted Maple Top), these instruments featured a beautiful 1/8" thick piece of solid figured maple that was hand bent to the top for the "perfect" sonic and visual compliment.

The new SCN pickups offered the player the ultimate in superior tone and flexibility. The bass featured a premium alder body with a bent, figured maple top. The neck was graphite reinforced maple, with a modern C-shape. The model was available with a rosewood or maple fingerboard, had 22 medium jumbo frets, and featured pearloid block inlays on the fingerboard.

It had gold plated hardware and the bridge was also gold-plated steel with string-thru-body or top load options. The saddles: gold plated brass. The pickups were the new SC-NLS J dual-coil SCN (Samarium Cobalt Noiseless) Jazz Bass pickups, and switching was done via a pan pot within the crown of the master volume control. The 3-band active EQ was also controlled by this dual-functioning knob.

The colors it came were Amber, Tobacco Sunburst (shown here) and Bing Cherry Transparent.

American Deluxe Series Jazz Bass® FMT & QMT V - These were the 5-string version of the American Deluxe FMT and QMT basses, featuring a premium alder body with a bent, figured maple top incorporating the Flame and Quilted maple tops (respectively) on the new models. The Hipshot® string trees with custom tailored break-angles were also used on these 5-string models. Specs were the same features and colors as the 4-string versions, the only difference being that thc 5-string came with a pao ferro fingerboard. Colors available included Amber, Tobacco Sunburst (shown here), and Crimson Transparent (shown here).

Deluxe Series Dimension™ Bass IV - The Dimension basses came from an idea that went back to my prior gig as the Squier® Marketing Manager. We had had success with the Squier MB-4 basses. In fact, the Squier MB-4 basses were still in the Squier assortment at this time and were still selling consistently. I felt that there was no reason why we couldn't build a bass decidedly unique from the Precision Bass® and Jazz Bass® platforms. We knew how to make electric basses since we had invented them and we truthfully had the tools, resources and knowledge to build anything we wanted. That was the beauty of working for Fender®, so we were able to effectively put this new Fender design into production.

The Dimension™ basses were made in our Mexico factory with all of the features and looks of today's modern-day basses.

The model featured a new Fender body design, with 2-on-a-side chrome tuners and a 24-medium jumbo fret bolt-on neck with a Pao Ferro fingerboard. It had an alder body and used a sealed P/J pickup configuration with an active 3-band EQ, master volume and pan control.

It utilized a new Fender top-load chrome bridge, designed specifically for this bass.

The pickups (also designed for this bass) were one Split SC 4-string P, and one NLS 4-string J.

Since we had decided to use alder for body wood for this model and we had Sienna Sunburst as well as Amber as colors, we needed to select the most figured alder available for use on these basses. Our team in the factory hand selected these body spreads for each bass.

The colors available with this brand-new Fender design were Black, Pewter, Sienna Sunburst and Amber (shown here).

Deluxe Series Dimension™ Bass V - The Dimension™ basses came in both a 4-string & 5-string configuration. The 5-string version was identical in features to the 4-string version, and it came in the same colors as the 4-string basses. The picture here shows the instrument in Black.

The pickups (designed for these basses) were one Split SC 5-string P, and one NLS 5-string J.

As with most basses I worked on, I solicited the help of some of our inside bass experts in the development of this model as well as *all* Fender bass models that I touched.

We had a strong sense at the time that this 5-string would sell as well as the 4-string version because players like John Myung were establishing followings as progressive 5-string players who played more "modern day" models. This 5-string model was perfect for that type of player.

One of our internal Fender bass-playing masters bought the very sample pictured here because it was exactly what he had been waiting for.

The Dimension Bass evolved further after my departure from Fender. It has been exciting to watch it change over the past decades.

Standard Series Stratocaster® Jr. - The Stratocaster Jr. was the extension of an idea by Todd Krause, veteran Custom Shop Master builder. He had built a smaller P Bass® for his son (seen on the following page). When he showed us what he had built, we decided to introduce this guitar and the P Bass JR. into the Fender® lineup at the same time.

Both of these instruments were built in our Mexico factory which allowed us to offer them at the same price points as the Standard Series of guitars and basses.

The guitar's scale length was 22.75", but aside from a single volume and tone knob, the features were largely the same as a Standard Strat®. This instrument was no toy. A simple hardtail bridge made intonation easy and these instruments sounded much like their big brothers. The idea was to create a professional instrument that could be used as a travel guitar, a couch guitar, or a guitar that someone with smaller hands could comfortably play.

As with the Standard Series, the features were 3 Std SC single-coil pickups, chrome hardware, a modern C-shape, maple 9.5" radius maple neck, medium jumbo frets, with a 3-ply W/B/W pickguard (our standard Fender spec). This model came with a rosewood fingerboard.

The model was available in Black and Torino Red.

Standard Series P Bass® Jr. - The instrument pictured here was the first sample of the P Bass Jr., modeled after Todd Krause's original bass that he had built for his son.

At the time, the only shorter scale Fender® bass that was available was the Mustang® Bass which was made in Japan. This bass was roughly 10% smaller than a Standard P Bass, but it played and sounded as good as its big brother. Its scale length was 22.59". It featured just a single volume knob and no tone control, but aside from that, the features were largely the same as a Standard P Bass.

As with the Standard Series of P Bass instruments, the features were one Split SC J pickup, chrome hardware, a modern C-shape, maple 9.5" radius maple neck, medium jumbo frets and 3-ply W/B/W pickguard (our standard Fender spec). This model came with a rosewood fingerboard.

This bass, although smaller, was one fully functional tool and quite unlike anything we had made up until this time.

It came in Black and Torino Red.

These instruments were released in January of 2004 but were only made for a couple of years.

Nashville: July 2004

Artist Series John 5 Telecaster® - Over time, John has become known as one of metal's premier guitarists. Like so many world class guitarists, when you start diving into the player and his/her background, you discover how truly versatile and gifted the individual really is ... and that is absolutely the case here.

Although known for his metal prowess, John can play *any* style very well. His playing history ranges from work with K.D. Lang to David Lee Roth, to Marilyn Manson, to Rob Zombie ... and many others. John first came to Fender's Custom Shop asking for a guitar and it became a regular Custom Shop pricelist model. Due to demand from a fair number of John 5's fans and followers, it became evident that it would make sense to release a more affordable version of his Custom Shop model. John agreed, and in July of 2004 we introduced this model. In dealing with John directly on this model, it became clear to me that what the world knew of John on the outside was a far cry from who John actually was on the inside. Mellow, soft spoken, highly intelligent and cool as hell ... these were my takeaways from working with him. And yet, when he plays, the monster comes out.

This guitar used the same headstock design as John's Custom Shop model. The reason John liked this headstock was that it gave him additional ability to bend strings behind the nut. We also used the same neck position Twisted Tele® pickup and a Fender® "Enforcer" humbucker in the bridge position. The model was available only in Black, with chrome hardware and a chrome pickguard. It was manufactured in our Ensenada factory and came with a deluxe gig bag.

This model was redesigned by John and Fender's R & D team a few years later, and the new John 5 Triple Tele Deluxe was introduced in January 2007.

American Series Telecaster® HS Upgrade - We had released the newly designed American Series Telecaster in January of 2003. Although well received, the one complaint we did hear about the guitar was that it had no pickguard. The fact of the matter was that we listened to our dealers and consumer feedback and implemented the change as a direct result of it — plussing in a 3-ply W/B/W pickguard. We had to be very careful whenever considering drifting from that common vision of a Fender Telecaster. This change took care of our player's cosmetic (and functional) request.

Since by this time we had introduced the S-1™ switch, we went ahead and added it to this model as well. The model still used the same Atomic II humbucker in the neck position, and one American Series Tele® single-coil pickup in the bridge position.

Standard Fender specs called for chrome hardware, a modern C-shape, maple 9.5" radius neck, and a model that was available with either a maple or rosewood fingerboard.

The colors available were Black, Chrome Red (shown here), Pewter, and Chrome Blue. The guitar included a hardshell case.

American Series Telecaster® HH Upgrade - The look and feel of a Tele, but a sound like a Les Paul? The American Telecaster HH was the solution. The Tele® HH was equipped with two of our Atomic II humbuckers and delivered a thicker, fuller sound than its single-coil predecessor.

The fact is that the American Series Telecaster® HH/HS – that were released In January of 2003 (shown on page 21) as mentioned on the previous models were in fact the same guitar. The change on these two models simply was adding a pickguard as requested by our consumers. We did that by adding the 3-ply W/B/W pickguard back to these models.

While traditional Tele players always have a "go to" Telecaster, this HH Telecaster was the another "go to" Tele for those seeking more aggressive humbucking sounds.

The HH was available in the same colors as the HS version which were Black, Chrome Blue, Chrome Red and Pewter. The guitar featured a W/B/W pickguard and came with a hardshell case.

50th Anniversary Series Golden Stratocaster® - Since 2004 was a milestone year for the Fender Stratocaster and one could only buy our 50th Anniversary models in 2004, I wanted to offer something additional halfway through the year to commemorate the occasion. Looking through old Fender catalogs, I kept coming back to this Aztec Gold '50s Strat®. Why not? Sure, it had been done before. But ... not only was it an eye-grabber but it was the proper color to commemorate the 50-year anniversary.

With this said, in July of 2004 we released it and produced it for the remainder of the year.

The specs and features of this 50th Anniversary Stratocaster were: alder body, 1-piece maple neck with soft "V" Shape, 7.25" radius fingerboard, 21 vintage-style frets, 25.5" scale length, gloss polyurethane finish.

The pickups were three vintage-style single-coil Strat® pickups with staggered, alnico magnet pole pieces, aged covers, knobs and switch tip. The pickguard was gold anodized aluminum and the hardware was gold plated.

The color was Aztec Gold, and the guitar came in a tweed gigbag. This was our final 2004 model commemorating 50 years of the Stratocaster.

Special Edition Series Jaguar® Baritone Custom - This was the first incarnation of the Jaguar Baritone guitar during my tenure at Fender. It was a good initial test, and it led me down the path to what would later become the Baritone Special, which was black and featured two humbucking pickups instead of two single-coil pickups.

Baritone guitars have been around since the '60s, with Fender manufacturing what was called a Bass IV. At that time, guitar players who were not comfortable playing bass, emulated bass lines by playing the Bass IV. George Harrison was seen playing one during Beatles recording sessions in the late '60s.

For starters, in terms of playability baritone guitars are strung with guitar strings. Baritone guitars rarely utilize the standard guitar tuning; players generally tune the instrument a perfect fourth lower than a guitar. The standard 27" scale length allowed this Jaguar to be tuned to B, E, A, D, F# and B which was the standard tuning for baritone guitars, wherein the fifth-string baritone E is pitched the same as the sixth-string low E on guitar.

Since this instrument was already being produced in Japan, it gave us the ability to bring it over into the USA and introduce it into the market. Again, a great way to test market a product with minimal upfront overhead.

The features on this model were: an alder body, oval or C-shape maple neck, rosewood fingerboard. 21 medium jumbo frets, 2 Jaguar single-coil pickups, 1 volume and 1 tone control, traditional Jaguar switching and Fender Japan's Tune-o-matic bridge. This model came in 3-color Sunburst.

It didn't last long, but it did give me direction in terms of what to do moving forward, when we launched the two new Jaguar instruments in January of 2005.

Anaheim: January 2005

Artist Series Eric Johnson Stratocaster® - In my years at Fender® and through the course of working on all of the models that I was a part of, one can probably imagine why this one stands out as my most cherished of memories. Fender had talked to Eric off and on for years about the idea of a signature model, but we officially got started on this project when we sat down and talked to him at Clapton's Crossroads Festival in June of 2004. EJ did not want this guitar to be a Custom Shop guitar. He wanted it to be an affordable pricelist signature model like that of his friend, Eric Clapton.

The problem was that in order for us to build the guitar to his exacting specs, the factory would need to purchase new tooling. This was expensive but signed off by Bill Schultz. We knew that the world had been waiting for this model and it was finally time to act. Rumors about Eric's meticulous nature had always run rampant. What I can tell you from working with him on this model is that he knows *exactly* what he is talking about. It was a serious education for me to "listen" and hear what he hears. It's hard to believe that a player of his caliber is this schooled in the knowledge of the nuances behind what truly make a guitar sound the best, but he is. Of course, respecting him as a player is one thing, but getting the opportunity to know him on a human level was a truly remarkable thing.

I worked closely with Michael Frank Braun (one of Fender's R & D gurus) who spent many hours with Eric on this project and was instrumental in getting it right. There are many aspects that make this guitar unique — as just one example, consider that Michael and EJ went through *17* different versions of pickups before Eric finally said "yes"! We had test guitars that we swapped pickups in & out of while evaluating the different pickups; a practice Fender had employed from the start. Michael started swapping out various EJ pickup "candidates" while I was playing and we were both listening. Oddly enough, when Michael put in the pickup set that EJ had just approved (though not with my knowledge), I quickly heard them and told Michael. "these sound the best to me." He just smiled.

Artist Series Eric Johnson Stratocaster® - The attention to detail that went into this model was immense. The things written about Eric I cannot comment on, but I can attest to my personal experience. That Eric's attention to detail in regard's to *his* guitar were very specific and we paid very close attention to his needs. We *had* to, or it wasn't going to happen. This model could not have fully come to fruition had it not been for Michael Frank Braun's personality and R & D expertise, paired with the relationship he established with Eric.

Some (but not all) of the details and features of this model are as follows: the very light 2-piece alder body is dressed in a thin nitro lacquer finish, and the 1-piece quarter sawn maple neck sports a 12-inch fingerboard radius, 21 highly polished frets and a soft "V" neck profile. Other features include staggered vintage-style machine heads (which eliminate the need for a string tree); specially designed Custom Shop pickups w/countersink screws and wound to Eric's specifications; highly contoured body and neck; vintage tremolo with silver painted block and '57-style string recess (with no paint between baseplate and block); four tremolo springs and *no* tremolo cover. The guitar came in White Blonde, 2-tone Sunburst, Black, & Candy Apple Red. This Eric Johnson model remains and has also expanded to include a rosewood neck version & an "F" style Stratocaster Thinline model more recently. This model came in a blonde Tolex G & G hardshell case.

No backplate (in case), extra trem springs

"EJ" Kokopelli neckplate

Classic Series 50's Esquire® - Prior to the release of this guitar, the Esquire had basically become a Custom Shop instrument. People had been asking for the Esquire over the years and we felt that it was time to make this guitar at a less expensive price point.

One might ask, "why buy an Esquire when you can buy a Telecaster® and get the additional pickup"? The same reason that Fender® invented the Telecaster® in the first place. Heritage, vibe and tone. That's why. The Esquire was originally played by some legendary artists and has been heard on many famous recordings. You can't argue with that.

Made in the Fender factory in Mexico, this guitar was introduced in January of 2005.

We emulated the features from the original with ash body, maple 7.25" radius neck, 21 vintage frets and vintage tuning machines. The vintage bridge pickup and 3-way "quick tone change" switch made this and the original Esquire accomplish its mission. The hardware was chrome, and the guitar had a volume and tone control. It featured a vintage bridge with steel saddles for tone and resonance. It came with a single-ply white Esquire pickguard.

The 3-way toggle switch gave the player three preset tones. In the bridge position, the pickup is only connected to the volume control (the tone control is disconnected). This minimal circuitry provides more top-end sparkle than that of a Telecaster. In the middle position the standard tone control circuit is activated, and it functions just like any other tone control. In the neck position the tone control is disengaged, but a tone-shaping capacitor is added that rolls off a fair amount of the top end thus accentuating the lower frequencies. This setting produces a darker tone along with slightly less volume. The idea behind this tone was for the player to simulate the closest sound possible to a bass, only played on a guitar, as the electric bass had not yet been invented. Originally, that was one of the motivations behind the creation of the Esquire in 1950.

This guitar was available in White Blonde, 2-tone Sunburst and Black (shown here) and included a deluxe gig bag.

Deluxe Series Players Stratocaster® - Everything about this guitar screams "workhorse Stratocaster." Since the new American Deluxe Series guitars were being upgraded with S-1™ switching and new Samarium Cobalt Noiseless pickups, it gave us an opportunity to use the current Vintage Noiseless pickups in other guitars.

Up to this point, the Vintage Noiseless pickups had been used mainly on the previous American Deluxe Series of guitars, but also used on some higher end models as well. and they had been made available as Fender aftermarket pickups.

Our first move here was to upgrade this model with our Vintage Noiseless pickups. We chose to use select ash for the body and selected a 12-inch radius neck. The neck was a modern C-shape, lightly tinted maple, and available with either a maple or rosewood fingerboard with medium jumbo frets.

The guitar also utilized a mini push/push switch that, when coupled with the standard 5-way switching, gave the player seven different pickup combinations to choose from. It came with vintage-style tuning machines, a vintage-style bridge and tremolo arm, a brown shell pickguard and gold-plated vintage hardware.

In addition to the pickup upgrade, we offered this model in new colors which were 3-color Sunburst, Sapphire Blue Transparent (shown), Crimson Red Transparent and Honey Blonde. This guitar was manufactured in our Mexico factory and came with a deluxe gig bag.

Deluxe Series Toronado® (Upgrade) - The slight upgrades we made to the Toronado were based on what people asked for with the current model we had at the time. We agreed and made these changes which turned out great.

R & D had just developed a new humbucking pickup, so we now had the Atomic humbucker to add as part of this upgrade. We had begun to implement this recently developed Fender humbucker into new models, and these pickups certainly gave the Toronado a more aggressive sound. As with all Fender products, pickups were evolving as well, and the Atomic humbucker, the Atomic II humbucker, and the Black Canyon humbucker were starting to be selected for use in upcoming models.

The upgrades for this model from the previous version were: a redesigned pickguard, new bridge and four control knobs rather than just one volume and one tone.

The Toronado featured an Adjust-o-matic™ bridge with anchored tailpiece. The guitar had an alder body and 24 ¾" scale length maple neck with 22 medium jumbo frets. It featured a rosewood fingerboard, combined with a 3-position toggle switch, and new matching black volume and tone knobs that controlled each pickup. Standard Fender specs are/were chrome hardware, a modern C-shape, maple 9.5" radius maple neck.

The model came in Black, Chrome Red (shown here), Navy Blue Metallic and Caramel Metallic. It came with a deluxe gig bag.

Limited Edition Series '68 Left-Handed Stratocaster® - With our factories in Corona and Mexico basically maxed out in terms of production and the demand for more Fender® models increasing, I had to look at other options. Fender Japan was always a consideration. It certainly didn't mean that everything they made was right for our domestic market, but it did lend itself to additional options to consider. There were models made in that factory that Fender Japan had tooling and parts for that we did not have in the U.S. at that time. This model along with the following seven models were new additions to our line-up for January of 2005. These instruments were made in our Japan factory and were part of the "Limited Edition" Series of guitars. In this case "Limited Edition" simply meant we would have them available for a limited period of time. I basically cherry-picked guitars that were asked for by consumers, but were not available to buy in the U.S.

This '68 Left-Handed Stratocaster came with an alder body and a maple neck with a separate laminated maple fingerboard. The neck featured a period correct headstock shape and logo with a 7.25" radius fingerboard and 21 vintage frets. It had three reissue single-coil pickups, a 5-position pickup selector switch and the standard volume/tone/tone control layout. In keeping with tradition, it used a vintage-style tremolo bridge and chrome hardware. If this guitar would have been available in 1968, Jimi Hendrix would surely have purchased it.

It was available in 3-color Sunburst (shown here) and Vintage White.

Limited Edition Series Stratocaster® 12-String - Twelve string guitars had often been used in acoustic folk music but it wasn't until the Beatles used the electric 12-string on some of their chart-topping hits that a demand was born for an electric 12-string guitar. An affordable, professional Fender® electric 12-string seemed like the obvious answer to that demand. So, Fender had stepped up to the challenge. In 1965 the Byrds released "Mr. Tambourine Man," which was the same year that Fender released the Electric XII. That guitar featured a Jaguar® style body and two Z coil pickups and filled a niche.

Fast forward a couple of decades, and Fender Japan began producing the Stratocaster XII based on a Strat® body and utilizing 3 single-coil Strat pickups. We had been looking at this model for a while and I finally decided that it was time to let the US market have access to it, so we brought it in and released it in the US in January of 2005. With the traditional Strat® single-coil sound, this electric 12-string really gave a unique and useful new twist on the 12-string electric guitar that other brands just couldn't deliver.

The features on this model were as follows: an alder body, a one-piece oval or C-shape maple neck, rosewood fingerboard and 21 vintage style frets. 3 vintage style single-coil Strat pickups, a 5-position pickup selector switch, volume/tone/tone controls and 12 vintage style tuning machines, a 3-ply aged W/B/W pickguard and an adjustable 12-saddle hardtail bridge.

Another unique feature of this instrument was the bridge. Six strings were back loaded through the body and bridge and the other six were top loaded through the bridge with adjustable bridge saddles for accurate intonation adjustment. This guitar resurfaces in Fender's product offering from time to time.

The colors it came in were 3-color Sunburst, Lake Placid Blue (Shown here) and Burgundy Mist.

Limited Edition Series 50's Left-Handed Telecaster® - The '50s Left-Handed Telecaster was built with all the appointments of a '50s Telecaster. The ash body and one-piece maple neck are the foundation for this modern music marvel.

Although the left-handed market is somewhat limited, I had a close friend (Brian Page) at Fender who is a left-handed player. He was and still is a great singer, player and songwriter. He was instrumental in persuading me to offer a 50th Anniversary Stratocaster® in a left-handed version. I heard Brian express his frustration numerous times with the limited selection of left-handed models available to choose from. Keeping that in mind, I knew that Fender Japan made a number of additional left-handed models that we did not. I had acquired several models for Elliot Easton (left-handed guitarist for The Cars) previously as he had encountered the same challenge. With these experiences under my belt, I always kept the left-handed market in mind and worked harder to offer instruments to meet their needs.

This model featured a one-piece ash body, vintage-style tuning machines and bridge, complete with steel-saddles, which added to the vibe of this guitar. The guitar had two reissue Telecaster pickups, a 3-position pickup selector switch, master volume and tone controls, and offered a diverse sonic palette. The neck was oval or C-shape and was one-piece maple. It had 21 vintage style frets, vintage tuning machines with a 3-saddle bridge and steel vintage-style bridge saddles.

The finish was gloss urethane and this model came in a White Blonde finish.

Limited Edition Series '69 Mustang® - The Fender® Mustang was for many players perhaps the first "real" guitar they had had back when they were first getting started. I know that was certainly the case for a friend of mine back in junior high school, for example. I recall playing his guitar and I thought it was cool, though I couldn't afford one at that time.

The classic Fender Mustang was another model that we rotated in an out of our assortment to meet consumer demand. It worked for us to do this with models manufactured in Japan, simply because they were already making them anyway for their own market. We brought this model back in for 2005. It was the traditional instrument everyone knew and loved.

This guitar was originally introduced in 1964, and the thing that made it uniquely different was the scale length, which was 24 inches.

Japan was using basswood to make these guitars and had been for a long time, although when this guitar first came out from Fender, poplar was used for the body. Basswood and poplar have similar densities.

This model featured a basswood body, oval or C-shape maple neck with a 7.25" radius neck, rosewood fingerboard, and 22 vintage-style frets. The pickups were two Mustang single-coil pickups (neck & bridge). The guitar had vintage-style tuning machines, a master volume and tone control, and an on/off slider, in/out of phase switch for each pickup. The guitar had chrome hardware and a floating bridge with "dynamic vibrato" as it is called, vibrato tail-piece.

The available colors were Vintage White & Sonic Blue with brown shell pickguard as seen here.

Limited Edition Series Jaguar® HH - This guitar was being produced at the Fender® Japan factory, sold to their Asian market. I felt that since it was already being made, why not try offering it to our domestic market?

While the basics were all Jaguar, the humbuckers on this model opened up new doors for players. The Jaguar HH combined the styling and functionality of a vintage Jaguar with a few modern touches such as the Fender Japan humbuckers. They were two special design MIJ (Made in Japan) HH Dragster humbucking pickups. These humbuckers made in Japan's factory were hot, with extra bottom end. The two Dragster humbucking pickups were the heart of this shorter (24-inch) scale length instrument.

The features on this model were an alder body, oval or C-shape maple neck, rosewood fingerboard and 22 medium jumbo frets. The pickups were controlled with 1 volume & 1 tone knob. The controls for the switching were as follows: "lead" circuit: 2-position tone switch, volume, tone; "rhythm" circuit: volume, tone, circuit selector switch; 2-on/off pickup selector slide switches, one for each pickup. That is the traditional Jaguar switching for Fender Jaguars.

Fender Japan's Tune-o-matic bridge with anchored tailpiece was added for tuning stability.

Topped off by a black with chrome hardware color scheme and a matching headstock, this Jaguar was very appealing to the rock-'n'-roll guitarist looking for something new.

Black was the sole available color in what Fender Japan called their Jaguar "Bottom Master" series.

Limited Edition Series Jaguar® Baritone Special HH - While the guitar market continued to change as it always does and guitarists were exploring other alternatives to create new music, 7-string guitars had already begun breaking new ground in music. I had looked at 5-string bass guitars and their suitability for these new genres of music but knew that there were also baritone guitars out there. With that in mind, we introduced this new model. An extension of the previous Jaguar, the Jaguar HH, this seemed to make perfect sense to round out this small series.

Like the Jaguar HH, this instrument featured the same two special design (Made in Japan) HH Dragster humbucking pickups. The instrument looked much the same, but the 27-inch scale length allowed this Jaguar to be tuned differently. B, E, A, D, F sharp and B was the standard tuning for this Baritone guitar.

The features on this model were: an alder body, maple oval or C-shape maple neck, a rosewood fingerboard. 21 medium jumbo frets, chrome hardware with vintage-style tuning machines. The guitar featured a Black finish and had the same cosmetic vibe as its "brother," the non-baritone version.

The switching was basic and simple: just a 3-way pickup selector with a volume and tone control. We didn't have a great deal of these instruments brought in from Japan, but we certainly satisfied the demand for those people who were looking for a unique baritone guitar.

Special Edition Series Toronado® GT HH - The Toronado GT HH was a version of the newly upgraded standard Toronado made in our Mexico factory. We were trying to keep the traditional muscle car theme in mind and leverage hotter pickups. You'll see the "Big Block" instruments covered here later. This particular guitar frankly went hand in hand with that offering of instruments.

While the "Special" or "Limited" edition designation of various models seen in this book tended to provide a clue as to the country of origin, that was actually never the original intent. It was more an "internal" indicator.

In addition to the racing stripe graphic, the difference on this model is that it now came with two American-made Seymour Duncan® pickups.

The Pearly Gates pickup is a great-sounding choice. By working directly with Evan Skopp from Seymour Duncan on these instruments, we decided to outfit these upcoming guitars with what we called the Pearly Gates Plus (SHPGP-1b), this pickup being exclusive to us for use on these upcoming models. The characteristics of this bridge position Seymour Duncan pickup were right on point: hotter-than-vintage humbucker output. warm and sweet tone with great sustain and a bright top end that really made harmonics jump right out of the guitar.

For the neck, we went with the SH-1n RP '59 reverse polarity pickup, which provides more midrange than a typical humbucker. The result is a neck pickup that cuts through with stronger tailored mids, an open and airy treble attack, and a warm, spongy low-end ... making it great for both rhythm and lead playing.

Unlike the traditional Pearly Gates, which uses an alnico 2 magnet, the Pearly Gates Plus uses an alnico 5 magnet and some extra coil windings. The SH-1n '59 uses an alnico 5 magnet.

The Toronado GT featured a mahogany body, had a 24 ¾" scale length, modern C-shape maple neck with rosewood fingerboard, and a contoured heel joint for easy access to the higher registers. Other features: chrome hardware, cast/sealed tuning machines, 22 medium jumbo frets, Adjust-o-matic bridge with anchored tailpiece, volume and tone controls for each pickup, and a 3-way pickup selector.

Complete with white racing stripe, this model was limited in production. The colors it came in were Red, Blue (shown here) Green and Bronze — with matching headstock on each.

Special Edition Series Showmaster® FMT HH - As I pursued my responsibilities to bring new products to market to satisfy consumer demand, maintaining the standards required to place the Fender® logo on an instrument was always critical. I always kept a close eye on the Custom Shop for inspiration. Whether it was viable or not, in my mind, my goal was to have instruments made that might approach something that our famous Custom Shop might create. In the course of that pursuit, I was frequently blown away with what our Korean partners could make. These Special Edition Showmaster models hit the mark at an attractive price point. While we had recently released the Showmaster in a few different versions that showcased different woods (namely: flame ash and quilted bubinga), we decided to add both flame maple and quilted maple tops to the mix as well.

These guitars had the same Seymour Duncan® pickups that appeared in the Toronado GT HH, those being the SHPGP-1b Pearly Gates Plus (bridge) and an SH-1n RP '59 reverse polarity in the neck position. With exception of pickups and top wood selection, the features otherwise were the same as previous Showmaster models.

Like the previous Showmaster, these guitars had basswood bodies although this time paired with a a carved flame maple top and carved quilted maple top, respectively.

Otherwise, specifications mirrored those of the earlier Showmaster: a modern C-shape maple set neck with a 15.75" radius, rosewood fingerboard, 24 jumbo frets and abalone dot inlays. The neck was a high access 25.5" scale set-neck (just like its brothers). It had smoked-chrome hardware, tuning machines with locking tuners, a 5-way switch, knurled knobs, a graphite nut and a 2-point pivot synchronized tremolo/bridge.

It was available in Natural & Cherry Sunburst (Shown here) with matching headstock.

Special Edition Series Showmaster® QMT HH - This guitar is the same as the flame maple version, but in quilted maple. The colors available for this model were slightly different, but the feature set was exactly the same otherwise.

Like the previous Showmaster models, this guitar had a basswood body — though with a carved quilted *maple* top this time.

Features and specifications mirrored the earlier Showmaster models: a modern C-shape maple set neck with 15.75" radius, a rosewood fingerboard, 24 jumbo frets and abalone dot inlays. The neck was a high access 25.5" scale set-neck (just like its brothers). It had smoked-chrome hardware, tuning machines with locking tuners, a 5-way switch, knurled knobs, a graphite nut and a 2-point pivot synchronized tremolo/bridge.

The colors available for the QMT were Black Cherry Burst & Tobacco Sunburst (shown here).

This series of seven Showmaster models — in addition to the two Tie-Dye models that we'll cover next — made for a total of nine models overall, and were the final Showmaster guitars Fender® offered at that time. Over the following 18 months, these Showmaster models departed the Fender assortment.

Special Edition Series Showmaster® Tie-Dye - These Tie-Dye Showmaster models incorporated new technology to achieve their striking appearance. The retro tie-dye patterns featured on these guitars were derived from real T-shirts! The graphics show so much detail that you could actually make out the cotton fibers from the original T-shirts on the face of the body and headstock.

I asked the Korean factory to design and voice these pickups specifically for this guitar, to help reduce overall manufacturing costs; and I knew at the time that this would be a limited run.

The features were the same as those of the previously-shown Showmaster models except for the tie-dye designs, the pickups, and that the fact that we used black hardware on this model.

We called the colors Hippie Blue and Band of Gypsies. They sold briefly — overall, a very-short lived model.

American Deluxe Series Jazz Bass® Left-Handed & Fretless - With the S-1™ switch, the P Bass® & Jazz Bass® had been opened up to additional variations on the traditional sounds usually achievable with these two bass icons. (The S-1 switching was explained earlier in detail.)

Because demand for left-handed and fretless bass models inevitably trends lower, we offered these instruments with a rosewood fingerboard only. (We consistently sold more basses with rosewood fingerboards.)

These basses came in 3-color Sunburst with W/B/W pickguard and Montego Black with a Gold Vinyl Parchment pickguard. Both models came in a hardshell case.

American Series Precision Bass® Left-Handed - When we introduced the Jazz Bass® in a left-handed version, we knew we needed a Precision Bass as well, so we pursued just that.

Keep in mind that this book covers and speaks of each new guitar and bass release in chronological order as these models were released in the Fender pricelists and in the *Fender® Frontline* catalogs for these years.

While we have covered the entire new American Deluxe Series of guitars and basses earlier, the standard American Series continued to march on "beneath" the American Deluxe. That said, this left-handed model was our freshened take on the left-handed standard American Precision Bass. The difference between the old model and the new model was the addition of S-1™ switching. By pressing the S-1™ switch, one could shift the sound of this P Bass® much more into the tonal zone of a Jazz Bass.

The model was available in 3-color Sunburst (shown here) with a parchment pickguard and also came in Montego Black with a Gold Vinyl pickguard.

Deluxe Series Active P Bass® Special - This bass was an upgrade to the current Ensenada-made P Bass® Special. The upgrade centered around two enhancements. First, we added the same 3-band active EQ that was being used on the current active Jazz Bass® at that time. And second: new colors! We revisited the color palette to give these basses a fresh new look.

The model continued to use standard specs: an alder body, a maple modern C-shape neck, a rosewood or maple fingerboard, with 20 medium jumbo frets.

It had chrome hardware with standard tuning machines, and a traditional Fender vintage bass bridge. The controls were volume, volume, master tone and active 3-band EQ with treble, mid and bass boost/cut; active/passive switch.

The pickups were one alnico spilt S-C P pickup and one vintage S-C J (bridge) pickup.

The new colors introduced for the model were Black, Chrome Red, Navy Blue Metallic and Blizzard Pearl (shown here). All colors came with a Gold Vinyl pickguard and each Deluxe Series instrument was made in Ensenada and included a Fender deluxe gig bag.

With the addition of the 3-band EQ, the P/J bass player now had access to all of the versatility that the Jazz Bass® players had.

Nashville: July 2005

Artist Series John Mayer Stratocaster® - The first John Mayer model was built in the Custom Shop by Chris Fleming. His signature model, made on our production line in the Corona, California factory, was this Artist Series John Mayer Stratocaster.

Although this project first began with meeting John at the Dallas Crossroads Festival in June of 2004 (at the same time the project with Eric Johnson began), John's signature model didn't actually get released until July of 2005. When an artist like John is at the top of the charts and dealing with pressure from record labels simultaneously, there is naturally only so much time available to devote to the effort — so it took a bit of time to hone in on and finalize instrument specifications to John's liking.

We finally got through those challenges and were able to release his model. One of John's heroes was Stevie Ray Vaughan, so when we sat down with him backstage at the Dallas Crossroads event, we grabbed Stevie's signature model and laid it down on the table next to us as a baseline of sorts to start the discussion. For me it was the ideal opportunity to capture the initial set of notes on what he wanted for the model.

Specs include an alder body with a maple neck featuring a slightly larger C-shape. The guitar had a satin urethane finish on the back of neck, a gloss finish on the face of the headstock, with a buffed finish on the peghead and a vintage '50s decal. The fingerboard was African rosewood with a 9.5" radius, and the frets were Dunlop® 6105 narrow jumbo frets. It had standard chrome hardware and Fender®/Gotoh® vintage-style tuning machine heads. The pickguard was 3-ply brown shell.

The "Big Dipper" pickups (John's own name for them) were spec'd to his precise liking and influenced by John's appreciation for SRV and the SRV Strat. The guitar had a standard 5-position switch and aged white knobs. It had five springs in the bridge block; the backplate was removed and came in the case. John's signature appeared on the back of the headstock, positioned closer to the "tip" rather than at the ball of the headstock, The string tree was positioned slightly closer to the nut.

We included an Incase® gig bag (as opposed to a hardshell case) as per John's request. The two colors it came in for its release were 3-color Sunburst and Shoreline Gold with racing stripe.

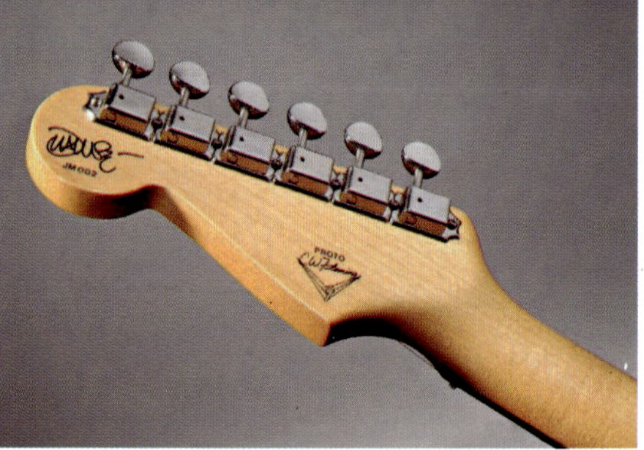

Deluxe Series Big Block Stratocaster® - Let's be honest: cars and guitars *always* seem to go hand in hand. This basic truth was a big part of the inspiration for the Big Block instruments (which included a Strat®, Tele® and P Bass® model.) Some people thought that the name was based on the block inlays used on the necks on these instruments, but it was not. Rather, the name is an homage to American-made muscle car engines — specifically, the Big Block V-8 engines in muscle cars of the '60s. I know *I* owned one, as many people did and still do. The goal was to create something sleek and eye-catching, with a bit of an automotive-inspired cosmetic vibe and a dose of extra output.

For cosmetics we went with a black finish, with matching headcap and vintage chrome hardware paired with a chrome pickguard. I looked at this as more of a rock-'n'-roll guitar, so we kept the controls simple with a single volume and tone knob. We went with a vintage-style tremolo bridge and a 5-way pickup selector switch.

Additional specs: an alder body, a modern C-shape maple neck, 9.5" radius rosewood fingerboard, 21 medium jumbo frets and block pearloid position inlays.

We used a higher output Enforcer humbucking pickup in the bridge position and two alnico magnet vintage-style single-coil pickups in the middle and neck positions. There could be only one rightful color: Black.

The Big Block instruments included a Fender Deluxe gig bag as these models were made in our Ensenada factory.

Deluxe Series Big Block Telecaster® - This guitar was the matching sibling to the Big Block Strat®. Nothing that looking like this had been built for the Telecaster previously, so it was a bit of a first across the board.

While all three of the pickups were Tex-Mex™ pickups, we reverse-wound the middle position pickup to eliminate the hum. More specifically, the pickups were two Tex-Mex vintage-style single-coil Tele® pickups with alnico 5 magnets (neck and bridge), and one Tex-Mex vintage-style reverse-wound/reverse-polarity single-coil Tele pickup with alnico 5 magnets (middle) which, as noted, helped eliminate hum.

Other features were the standard Fender 25.5" scale length neck, an alder body, modern C-shape neck maple, 9.5" radius rosewood fingerboard, 21 medium jumbo frets and block pearloid position inlays.

The model had vintage chrome hardware, tuning machines, knobs, a chrome pickguard and a standard 6-saddle string-through-body bridge (the same bridge used on the Nashville Power Tele). We kept pickup covers on the middle and neck position Tex-Mex pickups to match the chrome pickguard.

The controls were simple (as they typically are with the Telecaster): master volume and master tone with a standard 5-way Stratocaster® selector switch, operating just the same as a Stratocaster switch would.

All three of the Big Block instruments were manufactured in our Ensenada, Mexico factory. This model as well as the other two Big Block instruments came with a Fender deluxe gig bag.

Artist Series Reggie Hamilton Jazz Bass® - I had the pleasure of getting to work closely with Bill Cummiskey, our artist relations expert who had connections with so many artists. Bill had a long track record of involvement with the music industry, and people in the industry knew who he was. He oftentimes was the bridge that allowed me to get to know these artists on a personal level, so that I could begin working with them on their proposed signature models. Bill, Reggie Hamilton and I sat down at a hotel bar in Manhattan one afternoon to discuss working on a production version of Reggie's bass that was being made in our Custom Shop in Corona.

My impression in meeting and speaking with Reggie at the time was that he was a warm, up-beat person. And he is a extremely well-schooled player. The list of notable artists that he has recorded with and or accompanied live is simply too lengthy to mention. I could tell that his musical mind operated at an extremely high level. His roots were R&B, funk and jazz, and when you watch him play, he can play literally anything on cue with little to no rehearsal.

The idea (not unlike the strategy we approached other artist signature models) with, was to make a version that was less expensive but still met with the artist's approval. No small task.

The features on Reggie's model were: an alder body; a maple, modern C-shape neck with a rosewood fingerboard and 21 medium jumbo frets; chrome hardware; and an American Vintage Jazz Bass® bridge.

This bass had some of the same features as its Custom Shop big brother, like a Bass Xtender drop "D" tuner to drop the "E" string down to "D". It used an American Series Precision Bass® pickup in the neck position with a custom noiseless Jazz Bass® pickup in the bridge position. It also had a mini-toggle active/passive switch to engage the active pre-amp circuit. When switched to active, it allowed for control of the master volume, pickup pan pot and 3-band EQ with bass, mid and treble boost/cut. In passive mode it allowed for control of the master volume and pickup pan pot.

This model was made in our Ensenada, Mexico factory and included a Fender Deluxe gig bag.

Classic Series '50s Precision Bass® - This '50s Precision Bass was planned for release in April of 2005 when we showed it in January. The thought driving release of this this model was simply that since we already made a Classic Jazz Bass in Mexico, we'd pair it with a Classic Series '50s Precision Bass as well.

It was basic and traditional. It featured an alder body; a modern C-shape maple neck; maple fingerboard; vintage-style tuning machines and bridge; and a vintage-style '50s split single-coil Precision Bass pickup.

Other features included master volume and tone controls, a gold anodized pickguard and vintage hardware, very much a nod to its 1951 roots.

Though we know that the original '50s P Bass had a 7.25" neck radius, much like the Jazz Bass we instead went with our standard neck radius of 9.5" on this model. Everything else was period correct.

It came with a gold anodized pickguard and the colors produced were 2-tone Sunburst, Black, Fiesta Red, (shown here) and Honey Blonde. It included a Fender deluxe gig bag. It was officially released in the summer of 2005.

Deluxe Series Jazz Bass® 24 - Since the factories in Korea had capably demonstrated their ability to build excellent-quality Fender® instruments, I decided to give them a shot at creating a more affordable version of the top-of-the-line American Deluxe Jazz Bass that we had recently released. I sent an American Deluxe Jazz Bass QMT to our Korean factory. I told them I wanted this bass to "look" like its American Deluxe sibling, but that I wanted to implement some changes.

This bass featured a polyurethane finish on an alder body with a quilted maple top, and a modern C-shape maple neck with a satin polyurethane finish. It had a rosewood fingerboard with a 9.5" radius, and 24 medium jumbo frets (hence the "24" in the name). With 24 frets, that gives this particular bass a full two-octave range.

We used Seymour Duncan® Basslines single-coil Jazz Bass pickups, since we were now using American-made Seymour Duncan pickups in our guitars produced in Korea.

The controls were master volume, Basslines BEQ3 3-band active EQ and a mid-scoop "Slap" switch. Pickup switching was done via the pan pot, and the active EQ used a 9-volt power supply loaded with easy access from the back of the instrument.

The bridge was a steel chrome plated 4-saddle string-through-body bridge, and the bass had chrome hardware and knobs. We used licensed Hipshot® tapered shaft tuning machines.

This model continued to evolve moving forward and was offered until 2007. The colors it came in were Cherry Sunburst & Tobacco Sunburst (seen here).

Deluxe Series Big Block Precision Bass® - The bass brother of the Big Block Strat® & Tele®, the Big Block P Bass® was similarly muscle car-inspired and shared the same black and chrome motif.

The newly-designed humbucking pickup that we used in this bass was designed by legendary bass pickup guru Michael Frank Braun. The pickup was voiced to produce thick, rich, powerful humbucking tone that held down the foundation of any bass player's sound.
It featured an alder body, modern C-shape maple neck, 9.5" radius rosewood fingerboard, 20 medium jumbo frets and block pearloid position inlays.

It utilized a newly designed Fender top-load chrome bridge, previously seen on the Dimension 4 and 5-string basses. The vintage chrome hardware, tuning machines and knobs gave this bass a unique look with a sound to match it.

The pickup was controlled via a mini-toggle pickup coil selector switch. In addition, the bass had a volume control knob and a dual-function stacked tone knob that provided both treble boost/cut and bass boost/cut controls. The output jack was side-mounted. This bass included a Fender deluxe gig bag.

Anaheim: January 2006

American Vintage Series USA '70's Stratocaster® (Prototype) - Although the following 2006 models were released after I had left Fender®, I had them well under way prior to my departure. Justin Norvell capably stepped in to fill my shoes, completing development and release of these models. Justin's product development expertise through the years has resulted in some of the most amazing models Fender has ever released, and he will go down in history as one of the best to ever hold this role.

When this guitar was originally made in the '70s, it was built using either a 3-ply B/W/B pickguard or a 3-ply W/B/W pickguard. It was built this way simply to take advantage of pickguards that happened to be in stock and available at that time. When we did this reissue, I liked the B/W/B version simply because it was different than the pickguards on our other '57 and '62 vintage reissue guitars.

The '57 and '62 guitars were in fact exact reissues of exactly what Fender was making in the two respective years. Though I really wanted to include a '70s Strat® in this reissue series, it was difficult to pin down an exact model year based on the pickguard selection and yet still be truly "vintage correct," which is why we ultimately settled on "'70s Stratocaster" as the model's designation.

The guitar had a standard 25.5" Fender scale length. The specs were as follows: an ash or alder body; 7.25" neck radius; "U" shaped maple neck (gloss polyurethane finish) with maple or rosewood fingerboard; 21 vintage style frets; vintage chrome hardware, tuning machines and vintage-style synchronized tremolo bridge.

The pickups were three American made vintage-style single-coil Strat pickups with alnico 5 magnets and were voiced specifically for this guitar. The instrument featured the original's large '70s-era headstock, '70s style decal, bullet truss rod adjustment nut, 3-bolt neck plate with micro-tilt neck adjustment, and Fender/Schaller vintage "F" style tuning machines. Although it came with a 3-way switch like it did back then, we included a standard 5-way switch kit in the case which most players installed.

The guitar pictured here is the first prototype in 3-color Sunburst, with the B/W/B pickguard.

American Vintage Series USA '70's Stratocaster® - When this guitar was actually released, the decision had been made to call it a USA '70s Stratocaster and to not refer to a specific year as we had with the other American Vintage reissue guitars. It was, of course, built in the US factory like the other reissues and was slightly different than the '70s Strat® built in Mexico. It did end up appearing with the American Vintage Series in the Fender® pricelist in 2006, but (as shown here), and the decision was ultimately made to use a W/B/W pickguard instead of the B/W/B pickguard seen on the prototype.

I knew offering a '70s "reissue" might seem questionable by certain veteran Fender enthusiasts. Though the '70s were considered by many to be some of Fender's lackluster years in terms of build quality, the fact is that (a) the cosmetics and features were innovative, and (b) people still bought *many* Fender guitars and basses during this era. The fact was that players through the years had reacted well to this model.

Take "The Edge," for example, who had recorded many great U2 songs with his black '70s Stratocaster and has been seen many times over the years playing his '70s Strat live. And we're talking a guy who, in all honesty, could play *any* Strat he wished.

The specifications on the released model did not change otherwise. It had a standard 25.5" Fender scale length; an ash or alder body; 7.25" neck radius; "U" shaped maple neck (gloss polyurethane finish) with maple or rosewood fingerboard; 21 vintage style frets; vintage chrome hardware, tuning machines and vintage-style synchronized tremolo bridge.

The pickups were three American-made vintage-style single-coil Strat pickups with alnico 5 magnets and were voiced for this guitar.

It came with a deluxe black hardshell case (with orange interior), strap, cable and a 5-position switch update kit.

The colors this model was available in were 3-color Sunburst, Olympic White, Black and Natural.

This photograph shows a Natural example with ash body and W/B/W pickguard.

Deluxe Series Power Stratocaster® - The only true change in this model (which was originally introduced in 1997) was an upgrade in the colors that we were offering. And truthfully, it was *past* time for this refresh.

What made this guitar a "Power Stratocaster" was the primary feature that set it apart: the 12dB active mid-boost circuitry added to the guitar's electronics. This feature accentuated the clean and dirty sounds of the single-coil pickups and you could *really* hear the difference when you rolled up the tone knob. The first tone knob (meaning, the one next to the volume) is the no-load tone knob; and the lower tone knob (meaning, the one closest to the output jack) is the booster which kicked in the 12dB active circuit and increased in presence the closer you got to 10.

We used an alder body and the same features found in many of our Fender guitars: a modern C- shape maple neck; a 9.5" fingerboard radius (our standard Fender spec) with maple or rosewood fingerboard; chrome hardware; 5-way switching; vintage-style tuning machines; 21 medium jumbo frets; and a vintage-style synchronized tremolo bridge.

The new colors we released for this model were Chrome Red, Blizzard Pearl, Navy Blue Metallic and Caramel Metallic (shown here). It came with an aged white pearl pickguard and included a Fender deluxe gig bag.

Artist Series Tony Franklin Precision Bass® - There is a great deal that can be said about the amazing musician and genuinely wonderful individual that is Tony Franklin: but where does one start, really? In 2003, Tony came to work as one of our artist relations folks. After all, who didn't he know? He was stationed in our Corona, CA factory. I remember a group of us sitting and "interviewing" him for the job, already keenly aware of his ridiculous talent. He'd handled bass duties for huge acts including The Firm, Blue Murder, Whitesnake and countless others; his body of work is simply too extensive to go into here. Frankly speaking, he is known as one of the world's most accomplished fretless bass players.

During the development of his model, I got the chance to spend time with Tony and came to value him enormously as a human being. Tony owns many Fender® basses and has for many years, including a '75 fretless. In creating this model, he helped us introduce a true "Fretless Monster" in this bass.

His signature model bass featured a lightweight solid alder body, maple neck with modern C-shape, unfinished ebony fingerboard, and vintage '70s Fender open gear machine heads with a Hipshot® Bass Xtender for "Drop D" tuning on the low E string. While the P Bass® has traditionally come equipped with just one split single-coil pickup, Tony wanted his bass to have a Jazz Bass® pickup as well. Since he worked in our Corona factory at the time, as one of our artist relations folks (while still maintaining a busy touring, recording and playing schedule), he was right there "onsite" to work directly with our R & D folks in the development of his model.

The result were two pickups designed and voiced specifically for use on his bass. The Jazz Bass bridge pickup uses hex screw lugs and ceramic bar magnets. The 3-way blade pickup switch gives the player each pickup individually or both together. There are deeper subtleties in the way this particular 3-way switch works, like plussing in a capacitor and shaping tone slightly differently in each position, but let's just say this bass delivers a *wide* range of bass voicings, from vintage to modern. The Sunburst version had a brown shell pickguard, while the Black version came with a 3-ply black vinyl pickguard. An additional color was later added upon Tony's request: a color inspired by his personal "Baby Blue" bass which is Lake Placid Blue with a Silver Shell 3-ply pickguard.

Artist Series Frank Bello Bass - Not unlike any other artist series instrument project that we tackled, when I started to work on this project, the first job was to build some sort of relationship with the artist himself. That was not always easy — but getting to know Frank Bello a bit, absolutely was. He was a nice, humble man and a joy to speak with.

I recall meeting Frank at a show in Phoenix when he was playing with the band Helmet (even though he's most well known for his years with Anthrax). As we worked on this bass, it became clear that through all Fender®, basses that we had done, this bass was going to be quite different in terms of fundamentally combining Jazz Bass® and P Bass® features and incorporating additional specifications that really turned this bass into a true hybrid. This signature P Bass had a slab-cut alder Jazz Bass body, a modern C-shaped maple Precision Bass® neck with rosewood fingerboard, and a matching black headstock with a white scripted logo.

Other features included chrome Fender/Schaller deluxe Lite Bass straight-shaft tuning machines, a Badass III bridge, a "Fender Bass" headstock decal, and a Bello caricature on the back of the headstock (with his signature on the neck plate). The only onboard controls were volume knobs for each pickup.

The pickups were a Seymour Duncan® Basslines SPB-3 Quarter Pound split-coil Precision Bass pickup in the neck, and a Samarium Cobalt Noiseless Jazz Bass pickup in the bridge position. Though this model was short-lived, it was yet another truly innovative Fender artist collaboration.

Deluxe Series Jaguar® Bass - The idea that drove the creation of this bass sprung directly from another of my brainstorming sessions. And yet, I just didn't know if bass players would accept it. Fortunately, whenever I considered an idea of this nature, I had numerous people (and players) at Fender® that I would run the idea by for initial input. From there, if I proceeded, I would ask for feedback and possible changes to the working samples and prototypes of the model as we worked closer towards a finished product. In this case, the inside Fender folks were uniformly excited about the prospects of this potential model.

Once released, it ended up capturing the attention of bass players and the market in general because a "bass version" of the long-standing Jaguar guitar had never been done before — this was a true first. The instrument had the common feel and sound of a Jazz Bass® because of the body and pickups selected, but other than that it was truly a different animal. The switching, while not complicated, still needed to be well communicated and understood and we knew that going in.

It featured an alder body, modern C-shape maple neck, 9.5" radius rosewood fingerboard with aged pearloid block inlays, 20 medium jumbo frets, vintage tuning machines and a vintage-style 4-Saddle top-loading bridge. The pickups were 2 vintage Jazz Bass single-coil pickups, but the switching gave these pickups a lot of versatility. The switching functioned as follows:

Two on/off slide switches, one for each pickup, one series/parallel slide switch (operates only when both pickups are on). Master volume, master tone, preamp treble control wheel, preamp bass control wheel and preamp on/off slide switch.

This bass was made in Japan and manufactured specifically for the USA market, as Japan had never built this instrument before.

The available colors were Black and Hot Rod Red (as seen here), both with matching headcaps.

FSRs (Factory Special Runs) and Limited Editions

Factory Special Runs gave Fender® dealers the opportunity to get creative and design and sell instruments that were targeted for the customer looking for something unique and different. Though I recorded well over 100 Factory Special Run instruments that we made during my time at Fender, this book is primarily focused on our standard production "pricelist" instruments that actually appeared in our catalog. FSRs were made for different customers and distributors all over the world in both our Corona and Mexico factories. There were so many produced that quite frankly, an entire book could be written on just these instruments. However, in this book I simply want to provide a small sampling of the types of instruments that we did produce via the Fender Factory Special Run program during this time.

There was frequently a difference between FSRs and Limited Edition instruments although this was not always strictly the case, and it can truthfully be a bit confusing. More often than not, FSRs were models that were created at the request of a dealer from anywhere in the world. Limited Edition instruments, on the other hand, were more frequently created by "us" and/or were "my idea" and yet were still never intended to become a catalog and/or pricelist instrument for any length of time. This was a way we could test the market on a model, and if the response was overwhelming, perhaps consider bringing it into the standard Fender assortment. Either way, there were only so many made of FSRs and Limited Editions made.

The rules in requesting FSRs at that time were simple: an order was required for 100 pieces of American-made guitars and 250 Mexican-made instruments. The reason for this was that in order to make these instruments, Fender would need to plan for and set up production specifically for this run of instruments. Since the majority of product produced in the factories is core "pricelist" product and the folks at Fender are really the authorities when it comes to what should be mass-produced, these special runs tended to be just that: *special* and uniquely different from the norm in some way. To the degree of even being polarizing for the customer in some cases.

The additional rule for FSRs was that the requested guitar or bass could not require additional R & D. The Fender R & D department already had a full-time job just executing what was already on the table and was already booked many months out on upcoming projects. To involve R & D on a project meant initiating a new and expensive process. It meant new drawings, which involved engineers, potential new sourcing for purchasing to secure componentry, etc. New tooling costs for a new model was approved only when the corporate office saw fit to do so, as was the case with the Eric Johnson Signature Stratocaster.

Although this program was open to Fender dealers, I also would work with R & D to "brainstorm" our own Limited Editions and then offer them to the dealer base. All of these instruments were limited production models — in other words, we only made so many. As Steve Grom (retired Vice President of Quality Assurance) once said, "We don't just put a tree in one end and out pops a guitar at the other."

The following instruments are just a small sampling of some of the models we created via this program. Those individuals that own one of these have something truly special on their hands, because there simply are not that many in existence.

Limited Edition SO-CAL Speed Shop® Stratocaster® - When it comes to electric guitars, Fender's Custom Shop is second to none. Because of Fender's close relationship with the great people at the SO-CAL Speed Shop in Pomona, CA, the Custom Shop had built a guitar to be displayed at their corporate headquarters. The instrument was painted by the folks at the SO-CAL Speed Shop using their red & white colors and incorporated their logo. I had the Custom Shop build a second one of these guitars specifically so that I could send it to our Korean factory builders to see if they could copy the basic design of this Custom Shop gem. The instrument pictured here was the result.

We never intended to make a large number of these guitars and in the end, we produced around 600. They were never in the pricelist but did appear in the 2005 *Fender Frontline* magazine on page 69. Although the model was a fully functional guitar, most people bought this guitar as an art piece for display on their wall.

The paint job seen here on the front was mirrored on the back as well. Though certainly not a Custom Shop build, this model was executed unbelievably well and was an affordable piece of art.

The guitar featured a basswood body and maple neck dressed in the red, white and black SO-CAL Speed Shop paint scheme. It had a a bolt-on modern C-shape maple neck with a maple fingerboard, 22 medium jumbo frets, chrome hardware, tuning machines, a single volume control, and a string-through-body hard-tail bridge.

The pickup was a hot alnico humbucker. Even though a fair number of these guitars ended up on display on walls, the pickup had a lot of output and the guitar could really scream when plugged in.

Factory Special Run -'69 Tele® Thinline -
Although this FSR was essentially a classic '69 Tele® Thinline, the Arctic White paint template used over the natural mahogany body really changed the cosmetic vibe and made this guitar something special. In addition, to make the design really "pop" we applied a noticeable vintage tint to the neck.

So many of these FSRs or Limited-Edition instruments were visual "head turners," so to speak. They just really stood out and caught one's eye, yet are highly functional instruments.

The classic '69 Tele® Thinline model was always sought after, with the rich, warm tone of an all-mahogany body really complementing the Tele Thinline platform. The model has been a staple in the Fender assortment for many years and remains in the Fender assortment.

Though I intentionally do not mention the customer these instruments were requested by and made for, this model was out there for a short period and built for one of our USA customers.

Factory Special Run - Standard Strat® HSS Inca Silver - This FSR was a bit of a mix of a Standard Strat HSS, crossed with a Classic Series '60s Stratocaster. Based on the platform, this piece amounted to a simple color switch, pickguard modification and pickup upgrade. This was certainly not a difficult request.

This FSR was painted in Inca Silver with matching headstock, and it used a Gold Vinyl pickguard to give it a nice visual appeal. This color was already in use for our Classic Series '60s Strat made in Ensenada.

Besides the visual aspect of the color and pickguard swaps, "under the hood" we added two Tex-Mex™ single-coil pickups with staggered alnico 5 magnets and polysol wire, featuring a reverse wound/reverse polarity middle pickup for hum cancelling in positions 2 & 4. These overwound vintage-style Strat pickups increased output, sparkling highs and produced a very pleasing, warm tone while retaining typical Strat single-coil pickup characteristics. These pickups scorch!

The Tex-Mex humbucker, constructed with alnico 5 magnets, polysol wire and 4 conductor wiring, provided increased string response with a warm, full balanced output. The pole pieces are spaced to accommodate American Series and vintage string spacing at the bridge position.

This HSS pickup combination made this FSR sound every bit as good as it looked.

Factory Special Run - Deluxe Players Strat® Sienna Sunburst - One "golden rule" back in the day when it came to special runs was a simple one: the requesting dealer could not ultimately "own" the model. Meaning that yes, we would absolutely build it for them and let them run with the model as long as they continued to order it from us. However, if they chose not to order it any longer that was certainly fine as well; but that didn't in turn mean that we couldn't create something similar and introduce it into the Fender® assortment later. Naturally, as part of the manufacturing process we retained each of the detailed bill of materials (BOM) documents that went into the creation of the model in question. It was a rule, but I cannot recall ever needing to actually enforce it. FSRs and limited-edition instruments always just came and went, and that was that.

This factory special run was a simple cosmetic change. The difference on this guitar from the catalog-version Deluxe Players Strat was the color (Sienna Sunburst), and the white shell pickguard as opposed to a 3-ply brown shell pickguard on the catalog model that had just been released in January of 2005. (Seen previously)

Otherwise, the specifications were identical: Vintage Noiseless pickups, a 12-inch radius neck, a maple fingerboard with medium jumbo frets, gold hardware and vintage style hardware.

Standard Series Stratocaster® FMT - (Prototype) - Here's something a little different. I had had this guitar built, with the full intention of having it scheduled to be manufactured and released. That said, in showing it to our sales team, it was apparent that it simply was not sparking as much interest as I had hoped.

My thought was that the visual element of a flame maple top on a Stratocaster (as opposed to a Showmaster®) might be well received by the public. I kept the guitar simple, with a single volume and tone control. But, because everyone knows a Strat® should have a pickguard, it was met with lukewarm initial response.

The fact of the matter was that I/we were able to have literally anything that we could dream up, built and sent over for review. It was a wonderful creative freedom. However, that type of approach and thinking always needed to be kept in check, of course — not *all* ideas were good ones.
The colors that had been planned for its release were Cherry Sunburst (shown here) and Tobacco Sunburst.

That said, this guitar ultimately never did reach production and was never actually released. I've included it here just as a glimpse at yet another aspect of the role: the instruments that *could* have been, but never were.

Limited Edition '72 Telecaster Deluxe (Arctic White) - While we had already released this guitar in January of 2004, I had originally wanted to include Arctic White as one of the available colors. I truthfully did not anticipate that the release of the model would pose a concern in terms of insufficient consumer demand once we released it (and it didn't), but most other folks at Fender® were more cautiously optimistic. To be on the safe side, we had limited production to three colors.

The initial colors offered were Black, 3-color Sunburst and Walnut Stain. Needless to say, the opportunity arose to go ahead and release this in limited quantities in Arctic White, it was quite welcomed.

We built it and offered it as a limited run of 250, which we quickly sold. With exception of the color (which was my personal favorite for this model), nothing about it was different than the previously released model. The guitar shared the flat 12-inch radius fingerboard, the Wide Range humbucking pickups, and the Stratocaster® headstock of the previous model.

I'm admittedly proud to say that although this model has gone through several additional versions since, *none* of them would have been possible had we not introduced this model back into the Fender assortment, after being absent for over 30 years.

Factory Special Run - Deluxe '62 Stratocaster® - This model was based on an American Vintage '62 Stratocaster, and 100 of these were made in all.

I've mentioned several times that the Fender Japan factory had tooling that our Corona and Ensenada factories didn't have at that time which is why we brought instruments in from Japan. One thing they could not do at the time was use Nitrocellulose lacquer finishes, but our Corona factory could and had been for years. The fact is that the same held true for Japan. *WE* had and could do things that they could not. That said, we manufactured instruments in Corona requested by our Japanese partners.

The main "changes" were that it featured a flame maple top laminated over an alder body; and it had different pickups. Otherwise, it was very similar to a '62 American Vintage Strat® in terms of specifications.

The pricelist American Vintage reissue '62 Stratocaster used three period correct single-coils that were designed with special beveled alnico 5 magnets, a height staggered magnet array, and 42-gauge Formvar coated magnet wire.

This model, on the other hand, used a set of Custom Shop Texas Special™ pickups, with the middle position reverse-wound (as is typical).

The instrument was finished in 2-tone Sunburst with a nitrocellulose lacquer finish.

Factory Special Run - Gold Showmaster® & Telecaster® - We made this matching set of instruments for one of our customers here in the US and brought them over from Korea. Like the other Showmaster and Telecaster models we were doing at the time, these were also set-neck and had the same basic features and specifications, as previously shown in the Showmaster assortment. Overall, this was really simply a cosmetic change.

Like the pricelist versions, these guitars were made with carved basswood bodies, which were lightweight and very resonant. The set-necks were bound, and the guitars had crème-colored humbucking pickups.

We only made a very limited number of these, but they did certainly have an appealing traditional "goldtop" vibe to them.

Limited Edition Reverse Stratocaster® - In 1997 Fender® had created the "Voodoo Strat®" in tribute to Jimi Hendrix. It had been a USA model at that time. That guitar was, and still is, a collectible piece of Fender® history. The release of any product associated with an artist of this caliber is always challenging; there are always significant legal ramifications that must be understood and navigated to obtain approval to use an artist's name. It naturally helps when the artist can speak for themselves — but when others are speaking for the artist, it can introduce a whole additional layer of project overhead.

In this case, we simply wanted to offer a guitar that was reminiscent of something we had done before in the past. Customers had been asking about this for years, but in November of 2006, we worked around the challenges and produced a limited number of these guitars.

It was simply named a "Reverse Stratocaster." It was based on a late '60s Stratocaster and we had it built in Mexico so we could introduce it as a more affordable version of its discontinued older brother from 10 years prior.

It had a single-ply white pickguard and three Std SC single-coil pickups. We slanted the bridge position pickup to get the instrument closer to its vintage heritage. It is true that because of the reverse headstock, the different string lengths from bridge to tuner, and the position of the pickup pole pieces in the bridge position, this Stratocaster actually has a different (although still classic) sound. Like the '60s Stratocaster, this model had a modern C-shape maple neck and maple fingerboard, chrome hardware, 5-way switching, vintage style tuning machines, 21 medium jumbo frets, and vintage-style synchronized tremolo bridge.

This guitar was available for only a short time and was offered in Olympic White and Black.

Factory Special Run - American Deluxe Strat® HSS "None More Black" - Both this guitar and the "Bad Boy Blue" model (next page) came from Gary Waugh, one of our long time Fender® district sales managers. This guitar was based off of our new American Deluxe Series Strat HSS and used the SCN pickups along with the S-1™ switch.

Gary was one of the first sales managers who saw the opportunity to create a special release based on the recently introduced American Deluxe Series, and these two models were his requests. We used Gary's "names" for these two models because they were in fact fitting in their appearance.

The core of the instrument's specifications were very similar to those of the American Deluxe HSS Stratocaster®. This model also used an LSR Roller Nut, to allow zero friction on the strings moving through the nut when the tremolo is used. The pickups were a Fender DH-1 humbucking pickup in the bridge position, one SC-NLS Strat in the middle, and one Hot SC-NLS Strat pickup in the neck, wound *extra* hot for balance with the humbucker.

The differences were that this guitar came with an ebony fingerboard, had no position markers on the fretboard (just side dots), had a single-ply pickguard, and had a matching color headstock.

Factory Special Run - American Deluxe Strat® HSS "Bad Boy Blue" - This second guitar concept which came from Gary Waugh, was based off of our American Deluxe Series Strat HSS as well.

The pickups were the same used on the American Deluxe Stratocaster with an ash body: three SC-NLS Strat pickups. The guitar was also equipped with the new S-1™ switching.

The difference on this particular model was that it came with an ebony fingerboard, with no position markers on the fret board (just side dots) — and this model had an ash body finished in Cobalt Blue Transparent or in Gary's terms, "Bad Boy Blue".

If a customer wanted something different from the norm and preferred an ash body, this was it! In keeping with the special run theme, there were not many of these built. If by chance you own one of these models you may in fact own one of the only one's ever made and in some cases, it might be *the* only one that was ever made.

Limited Edition Antigua Stratocaster® & Telecaster® - These guitars were one of the first projects I worked on when I stepped into my position at Fender®. I had a friend that owned an original 1978 Antigua Strat® and Tele® that he had purchased together. They were in perfect shape, and I had the opportunity to buy them from him. I then sent them to our Japan factory and had them duplicate these instruments (something which they did perfectly).

Seasoned Fender fans know about these, and just how polarizing they are. They are not for the faint of heart, but, then again, music and the people connected to it are not "faint of heart" people. We released this limited run in the late fall of 2003.

Limited Edition Paisley Stratocaster® & Telecaster® - Paisley Strat® & Tele® models were originally introduced in the late sixties. Fender® Japan had been making them for years and we had brought them in to the US market here and there through the years.

The original "Summer of Love," as it was referred to, had happened in 1968. It was then that Fender had introduced the first Paisley guitars. Basses followed as well.

Here we offered them again for a limited time to satisfy consumer demand for these cool looking instruments. The same story existed for the basses as well but at this time we stuck to a run of Stratocasters and Telecasters.

Interestingly enough, those two names, "Paisley" came together in 2016 when Fender teamed up with Brad Paisley to create his road worn version of a Silver Sparkle Paisley Telecaster becoming part of Fender's Artist Series.

Limited Edition Rosewood Telecaster® - In 2004 I was advised that we had a surplus of rosewood that needed to be used. It sounded like a great problem to have from my standpoint. This rosewood was available due to the fact that we owned the Guild brand at that time, and we had purchased all of the Guild inventory — which included all of the on-hand wood inventory, both finished and non-finished. Now ... how to get the creative juices flowing and make something that would be appealing?

I spoke with Steve Grom (VP of Quality Assurance and long-time FSR mastermind) about this. He made the suggestion that we build this guitar, and so we built a sample. The guitar shown here is the result. We all know of the pictures and videos of George Harrison playing a rosewood Telecaster on the rooftop in London. That guitar was all rosewood and had a rosewood neck and headstock as well. The problem with building a solid

rosewood body guitar is that they tend be *extremely* heavy and don't sound great, although you certainly wouldn't know that when you heard George play. Instead of this approach, Steve suggested that we make the body of alder and use rosewood veneer for the top and back. Visually, one cannot tell the difference — and yet the result is a much lighter and (frankly) better-sounding instrument.

These instruments were a typical standard weight and sounded as good as any Telecaster made. We used Tex-Mex™ pickups from the Deluxe Series but a traditional bridge that at that time was used on the American Highway One Telecaster. The bridge used three-barrel brass saddles. We made roughly 700 of these instruments and when we launched this guitar as a limited edition, we sold all of them in a matter of weeks.

Limited Edition Standard Strat® HSS Aztec Gold - This guitar and the instrument on the following page were commonly requested and were based on the Standard Strat HSS made in Mexico. This instrument was a cosmetic change plus just a little more. Basic cosmetic changes were most of the time relatively simple, but the more we got into deeper changes, the more planning and scheduling was impacted. Naturally, we already had plenty of standard pricelist instruments to build as it was, so these projects were inevitably time-consuming in one way or another as they impacted a fair number of people, from the factory workers forward.

This instrument featured an alder body and used a modern C-shape maple neck with 9.5" radius (our standard Fender spec). This limited edition came with a maple fingerboard, 5-way switching, vintage style tuning machines, 21 medium jumbo frets, tuning machines and vintage-style synchronized tremolo bridge. Like our Standard Series guitars, these two models used two Std S-C single coils (neck and middle positions) and one Standard Series humbucker in the bridge position.

You will notice that this guitar was a little different because it only has a volume and tone control which meant it required a "not-off the shelf" pickguard. Aztec Gold was a color used to varying degrees through Fender® history, and we used it here with a matching headcap; we topped it off with a "mirror" vinyl pickguard drilled to accommodate just the volume and tone control.

Limited Edition Standard Strat® HSS Black - This Stratocaster® was based on a Standard Strat HSS made in Ensenada, and it turned out nicely. The aim here was purely a cosmetic change; experimenting a bit and giving consumers something a little different.

This Stratocaster also featured an alder body, a modern C-shape maple neck with 9.5" radius, a maple fingerboard, 5-way switching, vintage-style tuning machines, 21 medium jumbo frets, and vintage-style synchronized tremolo bridge. The pickups were the same as seen on the previous HSS model.

Black and Chrome always makes for a classy and purposeful look. With this model, we added a matching headcap, silver logo and engine turned aluminum pickguard, to really give it that "hot rod" appearance.

The factory special run instruments shown here give only the smallest representation of the many, many instruments that were actually built. Frankly speaking, almost *anything* that a person can dream up, can be made. The Fender Custom Shop was always the ultimate extension of that concept, and yet we managed to achieve tremendous variety from our production lines in Corona and Mexico as well.

Limited Edition '62 American Deluxe Stratocaster® - Prior to the 2005 January NAMM Show in Anaheim, I worked with Steve Grom to come up with a few American-made models that utilized the new pickups and S-1 switching system from the new American Deluxe Series. We blended vintage vibe classic models with this new technology, while maintaining the visual aesthetics of the classic icons.

The model on this page and the next were based on the '62 reissue Stratocaster platform. Like the '57, we used an actual color that had been produced in 1962 which in this case was Ice Blue Metallic.

Since the "theme" on these models was to combine the old with the new, these models used alder bodies. These necks were 21-fret and had a 9.5" radius, which had become a Fender standard back in the '80s.

The other standard for American Deluxe models was that they were finished in polyurethane. That said, we chose to use nitrocellulose lacquer on these limited production guitars. On the '57 and '62 Strat (pictured here), we used the vintage-style bridge and tuners to help maintain that "vintage vibe." This model featured a gloss light tint lacquer neck w/painted headstock, aged plastic parts and a 3-ply M/B/M pickguard.

As mentioned, SCN pickups and S-1™ switching were used on this guitar as well as the other models in this collection. This guitar came with a brown Tolex case.

Limited Edition '62 American Deluxe Vintage Player Stratocaster® - This model was a mesh of the '62 Stratocaster platform with the American Deluxe features.
This model differed from the norm in that we used nitrocellulose "thin skin" lacquer, which we typically used on the higher end models. We used gold hardware and a brown shell pickguard with aged white parts, as well as a gloss light tint on the back of the neck and the headstock to maintain that vintage vibe.

We also used ebony for the fingerboard making this a true mix of vintage goodness with new, modern elements. Like the other American Deluxe guitars, it used the SCN noiseless pickups along with the ground-breaking S-1™ switching.

This model featured a gloss light tint lacquer neck, aged plastic parts, and a 3-ply brown shell/white/ brown shell pickguard.

We also used aged plastic parts, gold vintage-style hardware and tuning machines, and a vintage-style synchronized tremolo bridge.

These "hybrid" models so to speak were hanging on display in the "back room" at Namm. We took dealers to this back room and showed our customers what they could get if they so chose to.

We chose to offer the guitar in Olympic White, and it came with a brown Tolex case.

Limited Edition '67 American Deluxe Vintage Player Telecaster® - In creating this limited-run of five guitars we took features from the American Deluxe series and combined them with elements from more traditional designs. This meant that on the "inside" they were fundamentally American Deluxe guitars, but on "outside" they retained the appearance and vibe of vintage, traditional iconic models.

This particular guitar did look an awful lot like a '67 (or '62) Tele® and it featured "thin skin" lacquer over Dakota Red on an alder body with binding. It had a gloss light tint lacquer on the headstock and neck.

This model differed from the norm in that we used nitrocellulose "thin skin" lacquer. We used rosewood for the fingerboard and kept with the Fender standard 9.5" radius, making this a true mix of vintage vibe and modern componentry. Like the other American Deluxe models, it used the SCN noiseless pickups along with the ground-breaking S-1™ switching.

This model featured a gloss light tint lacquer neck, aged plastic parts, and a 3-ply brown Mint/Black/Mint pickguard.

We also used aged plastic parts, chrome vintage-style hardware, tuning machines and a vintage-style Tele bridge with ashtray cover. The guitar came with a brown Tolex case.

Limited Edition American Deluxe Tele® - This guitar was one of my personal favorites, and we released it as a limited edition in 2005. This instrument was purely "American Deluxe" in terms of electronics, hardware and bridge. Really it was the Butterscotch Blonde finish on an ash body (much like the '52 Tele) that gave the instrument its vintage appearance. To further drive the point home, we used a single-ply black pickguard (also like the '52 Tele). Really, the guitar is a modern-day '52 Telecaster with all of the features of an American Deluxe Telecaster®.

Although the guitar didn't officially exist in the American Deluxe series, we showed and offered it alongside these other Limited-Edition models at the 2005 January NAMM Show in Anaheim.

This instrument featured an ash body with black binding, a modern C-shape maple neck and fingerboard, a 9.5" radius fingerboard, and light tint gloss finish on the neck and headstock.

As with these other Limited-Edition models, this Tele used the SCN noiseless pickups along with S-1™ switching, chrome hardware with locking tuning machines, and 21 medium jumbo frets. We used a modern chromed stainless-steel Tele bridge with chrome plated solid brass bridge saddles (identical to the bridge used on the new American Deluxe Ash Tele), and a black single-ply pickguard.

The guitar was available in Butterscotch Blonde, and it came with a black Tolex case.

Limited Edition American Deluxe Strat® Candy Apple Red - This was simply an American Deluxe Stratocaster® that had some attractive cosmetic changes. Also one of the limited editions that we showed in the back room at the 2005 NAMM Show, the color was Candy Apple Red, with a pickguard and a black painted headcap. Everything else was exactly the same as the current American Deluxe Stratocaster and it was finished in polyurethane just like the production line American Deluxe series instruments, so this was simply a cosmetic variant ... albeit a very nice one at that.

This model featured an alder body, and had a modern C-shape maple neck, a rosewood fingerboard with pearl dot neck inlays, 21 medium jumbo frets, a 9.5" radius fingerboard, and black gloss urethane headcap.

This model also featured black plastic parts, a 3-ply B/W/B pickguard, chrome hardware, locking tuning machines and a Dlx 2-Pt synchronized tremolo w/pop-in arm, as seen on the new American Deluxe Stratocaster models.

As mentioned, SCN pickups and S-1™ switching were used throughout.

This guitar was finished in Candy Apple Red and included a black Tolex case.

Limited Edition American Chambered Ash Spruce Top Telecaster® - We made a limited amount of these gorgeous, chambered ash Telecaster's. It had a spruce top and even sounded incredible acoustically.

Imagine what it sounded like plugged in? An American Vintage '52 maple neck with a 7.5-inch radius fingerboard completed the vintage vibe.

This guitar used the pickguard assembly from the American Vintage '52 Telecaster as well as the hardware and bridge assembly. Pictured here in Natural and Cherry Sunburst.

Limited Edition American Chambered Ash Spruce Top Telecaster® - Aside from the solid spruce top and chambered body (which was totally different from the norm), these guitars had the same features as a '52 American Vintage Tele®; except we offered both a maple and rosewood fingerboard.

Like the '52 reissue Telecaster, these guitars had a one-piece maple, "U" shaped neck (with nitrocellulose lacquer finish), a 7.25" radius, Fender® /Gotoh®, vintage style tuning machines, a one-ply pickguard, 21 vintage style frets, two newer American Vintage Tele® single-coil pickups, original vintage-style Tele bridge with 3-Brass saddles and ashtray bridge cover.

Pictured here in Black and Arctic White.

Courtney Love Stratocaster® - (Concept)
This guitar never actually came to fruition, but it did at least reach the "concept / ideation" phase and makes for an interesting story, regardless.

When I was working with Courtney Love on the reissue of Kurt's "Jag-Stang®" seen earlier, we talked about creating a model for her as well. She is really quite creative, and had many ideas. Courtney's management began faxing me her own drawings capturing some of the ideas that she had. It was clear that she was looking for a humbucking/single-coil pickup combination, with a simple volume and tone control. She wanted a hardtail bridge with a simple 3-way selector switch in the location that a second tone control would typically be located. She wanted the input jack placed on the side of the guitar to allow room for the graphics that you see here. She had drawn her own ideas for the graphics she wanted, as shown here on the original sample that was sent to Courtney for evaluation.

She liked it, but we never finalized the deal so no "final specifications" were established. Given the sheer number of projects that we worked on it was inevitable that some never made it to see the light of day, and this proved to be one of those scenarios.

Some great ideation and a fun story, regardless!

George Blanda Model - (Prototype) - Most people never put two and two together that George Blanda, one of our top guys in R & D and Dan Smith's right-hand man, actually had the exact same name as a former NFL football star who was a kicker and quarterback for the Oakland Raiders. That "other" George Blanda was inducted into the Pro Football Hall of Fame back in 1981.

The reason most people never made the connection was because Fender's George Blanda rarely talked about the fact that his father was that guy, the NFL star. Football was not George's life, however — guitars were, and his knowledge and skill were unparalleled. He contributed to many, many projects and ideas through the years, and was the brainchild of this model.

We always welcomed new and innovative ideas, and were always seeking opportunities to branch out from our widely accepted Strat®, Tele®, Jaguar® and Jazzmaster® platforms. This model is an example of just one such exploration, and the guitar was 100% George's concept.
We took this guitar to the January 2005 NAMM Show and proudly displayed it.

We were looking to gauge reactions from show visitors, and this model certainly captured a great deal of attention. It was a unique prototype and nothing like this had ever been seen from Fender® up to this point. It could not have been any further from the traditional Fender designs, and yet still had hints of its Fender "roots." We had used the phrase "Innovate ... Don't Emulate." for years, and this guitar fully captured that spirit.

The name "Axion" was under consideration for the model, as you can see on the guitar's headstock. The name is derived from physics and refers to a subatomic particle — not surprising coming from an engineering mind such as George's. I didn't get a chance to record the exact specifications, but I do know based on playing it that it had a 22-fret modern C-shape maple neck with an ebony fingerboard. Also, it utilized the same roller nut and locking machine heads featured on the American Deluxe Stratocaster® HSS LT, though the bridge itself was not locking.

Despite the initial attention, the effort lost steam and, although I continued to work closely with Fender after my departure, I never saw or heard of this model ever becoming officially available.

Bill Schultz

Bill Mendello, myself, Bill Schultz

Eric Johnson

John Mayer

Greg Koch

Tony Franklin

Brian Page

In my Office

Eric Johnson

Mike Lewis

Chris Gill

Jeff Carey

Justin Norvell & I @ the Cort factory, Korea

Fender Corporate Offices
Scottsdale, AZ

Credits:

This book could not have been written or inspired without my family — and when I say that I mean both my *actual* family and my large family of friends at Fender® Musical Instruments.

These people include:

Bill Schultz – Bill *was* the company and was everything it stood for. He essentially reinvented the company from the ground up and turned it into a thriving success story. As an individual he continues to be missed, yet still inspires countless people who have ever had the good fortune to meet and/or work for him.

Bill Mendello – Both "Bills" had to personally review and approve the transition from my former job at one of Fender's biggest customers, Musician's Friend, thereby opening up the pathway that allowed me to come aboard at Fender. I am forever thankful for that!

Ritchie Fliegler – Ritchie was the individual who took a chance on me in the first place, suggesting my initial hire for the Squier® Marketing Manager role. He is a brilliant man and continues to inspire me to this day. I could talk about Ritchie for days, but I won't as I'm certain that would be the last thing he'd ever want. Ritchie is retired from Fender, playing music and living life.

Richard McDonald – When I was promoted from Squier Marketing Manager to the Fender Marketing Manager role, Richard insisted (thank God!) that I sit in his office with him for hours each day to listen to conversations, watch him compose emails, take notes, listen to his ideas and thinking, and basically learn to mirror his overall approach. It was the equivalent of a real-time college course, one which taught me how to effectively develop and market products on a global scale. The baton was eventually passed to me, as I continued to learn. Richard is now retired from Fender, although still playing and keeping active as a business advisor and career coach.

Brad Traweek - Director of Fender.com, both now and back in the day. In addition to his decades of website work across the Fender family of brands, he also was strategic in so many ways and inspired me to follow through in the writing, editing, and publication of this book. Brad is an avid instrument collector and player and was also key in helping me reconnect with modern-day Fender to obtain approvals for the book. The era documented here overlapped the "early years" of Brad's own Fender career, and he has mentioned to me that he considers the models developed and released during this time period to be particularly near and dear.

Rich Siegle – Director of Branding at Fender. Along with Brad Traweek, back in the day Rich was overseeing all of the marketing content that went out both in print and digital form — not to mention the *Fender Frontline* catalogs which went out to all dealers.

When it came to obtaining photographs and supporting assets for use by dealers in their own marketing efforts, these guys were *it* and I relied on both of them heavily.

Rose Bishop – Rose was one of the best administrative assistants and finest ladies I have ever known and had a heart of gold. She supported me through many challenging times and I'm grateful to say that I worked with her then. I still keep in communication with her even to this day from time to time. The world needs more people like Rose!

Justin Norvell – There's *so* much to be said about Justin. He took over as the Squier Marketing Manager when I stepped up into the Fender Marketing Manager position. When I departed the company later, Justin assumed my position and took it to new heights. He still holds the position as Executive VP, Fender Products at Fender and oversees so much. Luckily, we still chat from time to time. He will go down in history as a staple at Fender.

Travis Kent – It got to a point over time where I really needed a personal assistant to help me execute all of the responsibilities needed to get the job done. Travis interviewed for the position; he was already in customer service and was also working toward a career in education as an English teacher. Everything about him told me he was the guy for the job, and so it was.

Mike Lewis – Mike was and still is one of my heroes. Before I ever came to work at Fender®, Mike had held the very job that I ended up assuming. When I first started as the Squier Marketing Manager, Mike was there to help guide me. I always asked for advice from the leaders there and Mike was a regular go-to. One of my favorite Mike Lewis quotes from one of those conversations was his advisement to "make it up and make it so."

Ron Kronewitter – Ron was such a great guy. He helped me immensely, helping me learn and comprehend my new landscape and supporting systems and processes when I first got started. He was running Fender Acoustic guitars at the time and knew the underlying how-to of the procedural workings as well as, if not better, than anyone else.

Brian Page – Brian was national accounts manager for our biggest customers, not to mention a good friend. Brian is yet another fantastic singer, player and composing musician as are many of the folks at Fender. He also happens to be left-handed. He has acquired quite a collection of left-handed instruments over the years. Most people don't know (because he is such a humble guy!) that he actually came in second place two years in a row on *Star Search,* the '80s version of *American Idol* ... but that's a whole different story and he rarely spoke of it. Brian's influence on me was and is both personal and professional, and back in the day at Fender® he was inspirational to me in introducing left-handed models into the Fender lineup.

Bob Willocks – Bob quickly became a friend and "go to" person. He did many things at the time including assembling all of the detailed specifications for all Fender instruments. Bob is a fantastic bass player, and there wasn't a bass that I touched without discussing it with him before I began the project. As the project would take shape, and samples and prototypes emerged, I always had Bob review them until we were ready to go.

Jack Schwarz – Jack has been a friend since childhood in southern Oregon. Jack went on after high school to pursue music and managed to make his way to southern California. He ended up going to work for Fender back when the offices still existed in Fullerton, CA. As he worked his way up within the company over time, Jack eventually became the SVP of Customer Service. When I accepted the position at Fender and moved my family to Scottsdale, I began working with my childhood friend from some 30 years earlier. Small world!

Chris Gill – At the time I was on staff, Chris was scheduling and planning the products we've covered here. He was really quite good at that. He was also (as many folks at Fender were), a really talented guitar player. Chris always gave me great advice. He took over Squier when I left the company, and created many great models as the Squier Marketing Manager.

Jeff Cary – Jeff and his family lived a few blocks away from me and my family, so we were neighbors. In our jobs at Fender, Jeff and I saw each other at work every day. Jeff has been at Fender for well over two decades and is now SVP of Strategic Initiatives. Previously, he had served for over a decade as SVP for Fender's "Specialty" brands, as we called them: including Gretsch Guitars, Jackson/Charvel (JCMI), EVH and Bigsby brands and related accessories. The portfolio of brands has thrived and excelled under Jeff's leadership.

Dan Smith – Dan was the head of R & D and spearheaded an untold number of instruments through his tenure. A true Fender historian. I spent many hours with Dan in Corona going through instrument projects in detail. I particularly spent an inordinate amount of time with Dan while creating the new "American Deluxe Series" of instruments in this book, although he was obviously involved in some capacity in every one of the instruments in this book. Dan is missed.

Andy Rossi – I first met Andy when he had relocated from New York and began handling the national account I had worked for in my time prior to Fender. After working with him for a while, he informed me that "a position" might be opening up at Fender. One thing led to another, and Andy helped get me the initial interview. The rest was history.

Michael Frank Braun – Michael was such a great force in R & D in Corona. And, like Dan Smith, he did so much with his knowledge. He could build an instrument from start to finish and had done that very thing many times prior to even coming to Fender. He was very gifted across the board and was instrumental in the development in Eric Johnson's signature model, among many other things. Eric liked him a lot and their chemistry made that model happen.

Brian McDonald - Brian was a good friend during my time at Fender, and still is. He was managing Jackson Guitars (owned by Fender) but, just as I did with many people at the office, I always enjoyed showing Brian new Fender samples so I could solicit input. I did this with many people at Fender as a means of tapping into the collective brilliance of the team.

Billy Stapleton – A friend for nearly 35 years, Billy is not only a great player and artist, but he has a vast knowledge of stringed instruments. He helped "coach" me in the creation of this book.

Evan Skopp – I had met and worked with Evan in my job prior to coming to work at Fender while he was VP of Sales and Marketing at Seymour Duncan, so getting the chance to continue working with him at Fender while developing models for our assortment was fun. I had him review these models that we worked on together to make sure everything was correct. Evan is a great guy.

Jill Layton – Jill was instrumental in helping source and establish connections with both Ron & Jeremey who in turn became involved as you can see below. Jill inspired and pushed to get this book available to print.

Ron "Crafty" Craft – Ron was the man who helped "create" the visual aspects of this book such as the front, back and spindle as well as the initial layout and templates needed to create this book. He also was responsible for cleaning up, formatting, and preparing the imagery that appears throughout the book.

Jeremy Sinks – Jeremy created the "internal" book layouts and templates needed to create this book. He also was responsible for cleaning up, formatting, and the preparation for this book to go to print.

Jon Varo and Michael Roberts – Current members of Fender's product information management team who assisted us in tracking down a few missing product images. Thank you, gents!

Kevin Fallon – Kevin, who was once my boss and managed the largest music store in Seattle when I was young, became my close friend and has remained so for over 35 years. He is schooled and an English major. With these tools and his tremendous knowledge, Kevin became the editor and coach for this book and held my feet to the fire to make sure everything was correct. Thank you, Kevin!

My Family – My father, Harvey Tonn, was particularly excited about this book and watched as it was written. He told me as he always has, "we never quit". My mother. She could see that as a kid, my eyes lit up when music was being played. She took me to the movies to see "Tommy" when I was ten. She also took me to my first concert when I was 12 years old. We saw The Guess Who and that was it. I never put the guitar down after that. My mother supported my musical career my entire life, like wonderful parents do. Robin and Mackenzie, my family at the time who made the journey to Fender with me. My daughter, Mackenzie Tonn, was just 3 years old when the "era" documented here was happening — she is my everything and will be until I'm gone! Mackenzie has always inspired me to push forward in the creation and completion of this book, the writing and recording of my own music and inspiration in life.

More Great Books from Centerstream...

COWBOY GUITARS

by Steve Evans and Ron Middlebrook
foreword by Roy Rogers, Jr.

Back in the good old days, all of America was infatuated with the singing cowboys of movies and radio. This huge interest led to the production of "cowboy guitars." This fun, fact-filled book is an outstanding roundup of these wonderful instruments.

00000281 Softcover (232 pages) $35.00
00000303 Hardcover (234 pages) $55.00

THE GIBSON 'BURST
1958-1960

by Jay Scott and Vic DaPra
forewords by Jimmy Page and Robby Krieger

A musical instrument or a cultural icon? Certainly, the Gibson Les Paul "Sunburst" Standard has become the single most desirable and collectable electric guitar ever made. The late '50s middle-of-the-road guitar emerges as the turn-of-the-century Holy Grail. With over 300 'Bursts shown and 16 pages of full color photos, this is the book for all collectors. Also includes a 1958, '59, and '60 Sunburst Les Paul serial number list.

"Since the first publication of this book 'til today, the Sunburst has continued to inspire me and new generations of musicians. Thank you, Les."
– Jimmy Page

00000423 Softcover $35.00
00000477 Hardcover $50.00

THE GIBSON 175
Its History and Its Players

by Adrian Ingram

Debuting in 1949 and in continuous production ever since, the ES-175 is one of the most versatile and famous guitars in music history. The first Gibson electric to feature a Florentine cutaway, the ES-175 was also one of the first Electric Spanish guitars to be fitted with P.A.F. humbuckers and is prized for its playability, craftsmanship, and full rich tone. Written by noted author/guitarist Adrian Ingram, contents include: the complete history of the 175, The Players, a beautiful ES-175 Color Gallery, Chronology, Shipping Totals, and more. This book is a must for every guitar player and enthusiast or collector.

00001134 .... $24.95

THE GIBSON 335
Its History and Its Players

by Adrian Ingram

Gibson's first "semi-acoustic" the ES-335, which was neither totally solid nor fully acoustic, is the guitar of choice used by many famous guitarists such as Andy Summers, Elvin Bishop, Lee Ritenour, Jay Graydon, Robben Ford, Freddie King, John McLaughin, Jimmy Page, Chuck Berry, Tony Mottola, Johnny Rivers, Jack Wilkins, Bono, Grant Green, Eric Clapton, Stevie Ray Vaughan, Alvin Lee, B.B. King, Emily Remler, Otis Rush, Pete Townshend, John Lee Hooker, and Larry Carlton. This book includes the complete history of the 335, the players, a beautiful color section, chronology, shipping totals and more. A must-have for every 335 player and guitar enthusiast or collector!

00000353 120 pages $29.95

THE GIBSON L5

by Adrian Ingram

Introduced in 1922, the Gibson L5 is the precursor of the modern archtop guitar. This book takes a look at its history and most famous players, from its creation, through the Norlin years, to its standing today as the world's most popular jazz guitar. Includes a 16-page full color photo section.

00000216 112 pages $29.95

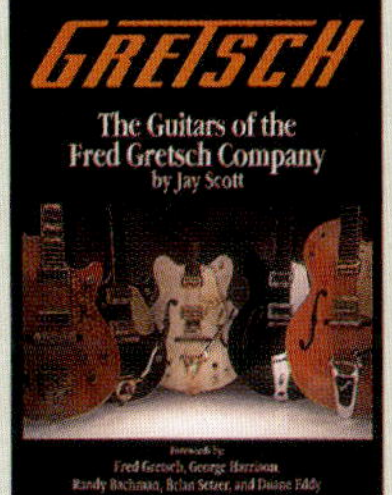

GRETSCH – THE GUITARS OF THE FRED GRETSCH COMPANY

by Jay Scott

This comprehensive manual uncovers the history of Gretsch guitars through 32 pages of color photos, hundreds of black & white photos, and forewords by Fred Gretsch, George Harrison, Randy Bachman, Brian Setzer, and Duane Eddy. It covers each model in depth, including patent numbers and drawings for collectors.

00000142 286 pages $35.00

THE HISTORY & ARTISTRY OF NATIONAL RESONATOR INSTRUMENTS

by Bob Brozman

This book is a history book, source book and owner's manual for players and fans that covers the facts and figures necessary for serious collectors. In addition to many black and white historical photos, there is a 32-page color section, and appendixes with serial numbers for all instruments, a company chronology, and a Hawaiian Artist Discography.

00000154 296 pages $35.00

P.O. Box 17878 - Anaheim Hills, CA 92817
(714) 779-9390 www.centerstream-usa.com

More Great Books from Centerstream...

LAP STEEL GUITAR

by Andy Volk

This first-ever comprehensive book about lap-steel and console steel guitars includes: interviews and profiles of more than 35 of the greatest electric and acoustic steel guitarists of the past and present, representing most forms of music played in the world today. Also includes resources for guitars, amplifiers, accessories, instructional materials, steel guitar tunings; and much more.

00000320 336 pages $35.00

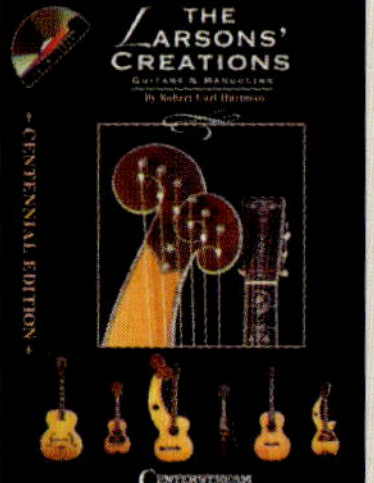

THE LARSONS' CREATIONS – CENTENNIAL EDITION

Guitars & Mandolins

by Robert Carl Hartman

This book is an account of two brothers who were premier producers of stringed instruments in the early part of this century. Swedish immigrant cabinet makers Carl and August Larson made instruments under the brand names of Maurer, Prairie State, Euphonon, W.J. Dyer & Bro., Wm. C. Stahl, and under their own name, and their highly collectible creations are considered today to be some of the finest ever made. This volume includes 16 pages of full-color photos, classic advertisements and catalogs, and a CD featuring guitarist Muriel Anderson playing 11 songs on 11 Larson instruments.

00001043 Hardcover Book/CD Pack $65.00
00001042 Softcover Book/CD Pack $45.00

MAKING AN ARCHTOP GUITAR

by Robert Benedetto

The definitive work on the design and construction of an acoustic archtop guitar by one of the most talented luthiers of the twentieth century. Benedetto shows all aspects of construction, even through marketing your finished work. Includes a list of suppliers; a list of serial numbers for Benedetto guitars; full-color plates; photos from the author's personal scrapbook; and fold-out templates.

00000174 260 pages $39.95

MUSIC MAN: 1978 TO 1982 (AND THEN SOME!)

The Other Side of the Story

by Frank W/M Green

Legendary for their construction and longevity, Music Man amps have earned the trust and respect of musicians worldwide. The company was the brainchild of industry vets Leo Fender, Forrest White, and Tom Walker. This book examines the latter – the company's "genius chief pilot/navigator" – particularly during the productive epoch from 1978 to 1982.

00001100 .... $24.95

PICKUPS, WINDINGS AND MAGNETS

... And the Guitar Became Electric

by Mario Milan

Guitar collectors rejoice! The first book to examine pickups in detail is here! Covers everything from the first experiments to classic models conceived for Rickenbacker, Gibson, Fender, Gretsch, Danelectro, Epiphone, and others, with an overview of Japanese and European manufacturers. Includes a 32-page color section of the most popular models and rarities, a timeline, info on building pickups and technical specs, and biographical notes on George Beauchamp, Leo Fender, Seth Lover, Larry DiMarzio, and Seymour Duncan.

00001026 .... $29.95

RICKENBACKER

by Richard Smith

A complete and illustrated history of the development of Rickenbacker instruments from 1931 to the present, complete with information and full-color photos of the many Rickenbacker artists.

00000098 256 pages $35.00

WASHBURN PREWAR INSTRUMENT STYLES

Guitars, Mandolins, Banjos and Ukuleles 1883-1940

By Hubert Pleijsier

The vintage guitar collecting market continues to grow. This book is the first of its kind to report on pre-war Washburn guitars, mandolins, banjos and ukuleles. It contains detailed information about more than 450 instrument styles, serial numbering schemes and estimated production totals. A gorgeous 32-page color photo section of the most collectibles will make this book a "must" for players and collectors alike.

00001176 272 pages $45.00

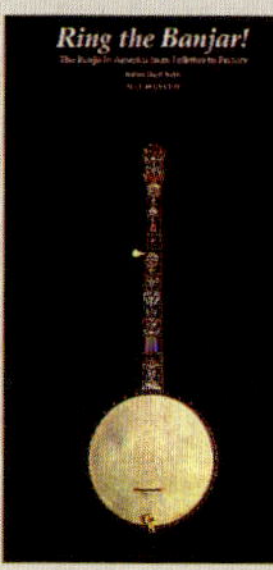

RING THE BANJAR!

The Banjo in America from Folklore to Factory

by Robert Lloyd Webb

This is a second edition of a publication originally published to coincide with an exhibition of the same name at the Massachusetts Institute of Technology Museum. Includes information on the banjo's enduring popularity, the banjo makers of Boston, instruments from the exhibition, a glossary and bibliography of the banjo, and more.

00000087 102 pages $24.95

P.O. Box 17878 - Anaheim Hills, CA 92817

(714) 779-9390 www.centerstream-usa.com

Are You a Believer? If So, Check Out Burst Believers I through V

BURST BELIEVERS
by Vic DaPra
00117070........................ $59.99

BURST BELIEVERS II
by Vic DaPra
00139084........................ $69.99

BURST BELIEVERS III
by Vic DaPra
00218000........................ $85.00

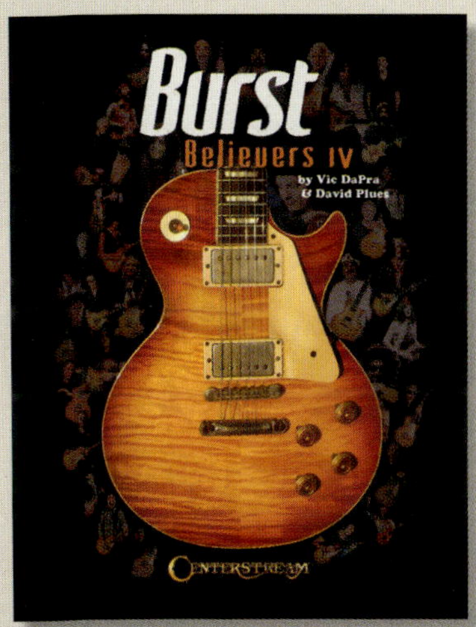

BURST BELIEVERS IV
by Vic Da Pra & David Plues
00287873........................ $85.00

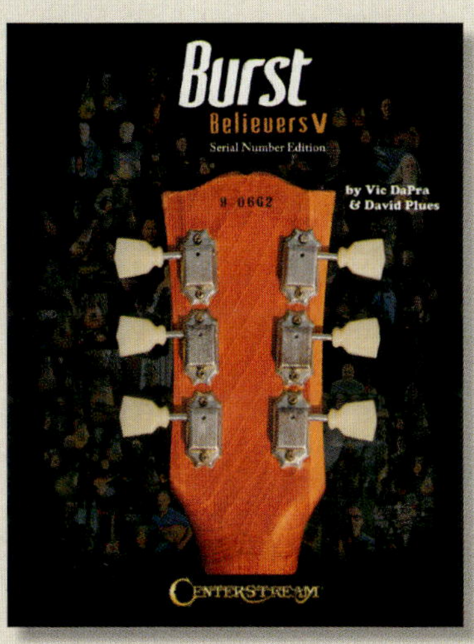

BURST BELIEVERS V
by Vic Da Pra & David Plues
00350746........................ $85.00

BURST BELIEVERS 2-BOOK SET
by Vic DaPra
00140979 Hardcover, 2 Books........ $175.00

P.O. Box 17878 - Anaheim Hills, CA 92817
(714) 779-9390 www.centerstream-usa.com

Those using
Centerstream
Books & DVDs

The Competition